# Brilliant
# New CLAIT 2006

## Jackie Sherman

PEARSON
Prentice
Hall

Harlow, England • London • New York • Boston • San Francisco • Toronto
Sydney • Tokyo • Singapore • Hong Kong • Seoul • Taipei • New Delhi
Cape Town • Madrid • Mexico City • Amsterdam • Munich • Paris • Milan

**Pearson Education Limited**
Edinburgh Gate
Harlow
Essex CM20 2JE
England

and Associated Companies throughout the world

*Visit us on the World Wide Web at*:
www.pearsoned.co.uk

First published 2008

ISBN: 978-0-13-615794-6

**British Library Cataloguing-in-Publication Data**
A catalogue record for this book is available from the British Library

10 9 8 7 6 5 4 3 2 1
11 10 09 08 07

Typeset in 9/12pt Helvetica Roman by 30
Printed by Ashford Colour Press Ltd., Gosport

*The publisher's policy is to use paper manufactured from sustainable forests.*

# Contents

## 5 Working with Documents 36

# 5 Saving and Printing

## UNIT 3  DATABASE MANIPULATION

## UNIT 4  PRODUCING AN E-PUBLICATION

## 4 Saving and Printing a Publication 183

## UNIT 5 CREATING AN E-PRESENTATION

## 1 Using PowerPoint 189

## 2 Text 196

## UNIT 6 E-IMAGE CREATION

## UNIT 8  ONLINE COMMUNICATION

# Introduction

## Who is this book for?

This book is designed to teach you everything you need to know to gain the New CLAIT 2006 qualification. With a wide choice of units that you can take, the eight main units are all covered in depth.

It assumes that you will be using Microsoft Office XP (2002) software and will be working on a machine running the Windows XP operating system. All the screenshots will reflect this, so if you have different software, you may still find the contents helpful but your screen could look rather different. One unit also requires knowledge of an image editing package. This book uses Paint Shop Pro for the examples.

## How this book works

The book covers all the assessment objectives included in the New CLAIT 2006 syllabus, including the knowledge, skills and understanding that will be tested. Each objective will be highlighted in the book (shown in the form [Assessment Objective 2b]) so you can be quite sure that, if you work through the entire book carefully, you will not leave any gaps. Every skill will be explained with step-by-step instructions and illustrations of what you will see on screen. You will also be provided with alternative methods for carrying out many of the tasks as you will soon find that there is more than one way to do anything on a computer.

New CLAIT is either assessed online or you hand in paper printouts of your work. You are allowed up to four data entry or accuracy errors for each unit, but there are certain errors regarded as *critical* which will result in an instant fail. All critical errors are highlighted in the text, and common mistakes made by students are also indicated, so that you are aware of them and can avoid making them when it comes to taking any of the assessments.

One critical error that is relevant to all units is a missing printout. Without the evidence that you have followed the instructions and carried out a specified task, you cannot pass. Make sure that you hand in *all* the necessary printouts at the end of any assessment.

If you want to practise using your computing skills and knowledge in preparation for the assessments, you will find a wide range of exercises available in *Practical Exercises for New CLAIT 2006*, published by Pearson Prentice Hall.

# Acknowledgements

We are grateful to the following for permission to reproduce copyright material:

(Page 279) Southcorp Wines Pty Ltd for web page screenshot from Australian Wines of Distinction, www.australianwines.com.au; (Page 302) Dr Luis Francisco Cordero for Christmas tree photo, as featured on the www.sxc.hu/photo/677681 web page; (Page 304) Hub Management for web page screenshot from www.browseforbooks.com; and (Page 312) Visualsoft UK Ltd for web page screenshot from www.piedog.com, © Visualsoft UK Ltd, www.visualsoft.co.uk. The screenshots in this book are reprinted by permission of Microsoft Corporation.

In some instances we have been unable to trace the owners of copyright material, and we would appreciate any information that would enable us to do so.

## Learning outcomes

At the end of this unit, you should be able to:

- → Identify and use a computer workstation and appropriate system software
- → Use a computer's system software to create and manage files and folders
- → Identify and use word processing software correctly to enter text, numbers and symbols accurately
- → Format basic paragraph and document properties

# CHAPTER 1

# Using a Computer

**1**

## What You'll Do

→ Discover computers

→ Distinguish between hardware and software

→ Work safely with computers

→ Discover the desktop

→ Change basic settings

## 1.1 Computers

### 1.1.1 What is a Computer?

**Assessment Objective 1**

A computer is an electronic machine for storing and processing information. Most everyday computers are made up of the following components: a central processing unit (the CPU); the main memory (RAM – Random Access Memory); disk drives for storing information; a keyboard for inputting instructions; and a monitor or screen for the display.

You may work on one of two types of computer: a desktop or personal computer (a PC) that normally sits on a desk, or a laptop or notebook computer that can be easily moved around or taken on journeys.

## 1.2 Hardware and Software

### 1.2.1 What is Hardware?

Any parts of a computer system that can be seen or touched are referred to as hardware. These will include the main unit housing the CPU and disk drives; the keyboard; the monitor; the mouse; cables; and extra items known as peripherals such as printers, scanners, speakers etc. necessary for carrying out particular tasks.

### 1.2.2 Working with a Mouse

A computer can be given instructions by pressing keys on a keyboard or buttons on a mouse. There are usually two buttons on the top of the mouse:

- Press the left button once (known as clicking) to select an item on screen such as an option on a menu.

- Press the left button twice, very fast (known as double clicking), to select and then complete an action such as opening a program.

- Press the right button once (known as right clicking) to open a menu of options.

A modern mouse may also have a central button known as the scroll wheel. Pressing this and then dragging the mouse will move the display up or down the screen.

**What if I find it hard to double click?**

You can click once with the left mouse button and then press the Enter key on the keyboard instead.

### 1.2.3 What is Software?

This is the general name for programs that are run on the computer. There are two main types of software:

- Systems software: this includes the programs known as the operating system controlling the computer. You may come across Windows, Mac or Linux.

- Applications software: these are programs designed to carry out particular tasks such as word processing, desktop publishing or image editing. This book will introduce you to a number of applications including Microsoft Word, Excel and FrontPage.

## 1.3 Working Safely with Computers

### 1.3.1 Why it Matters

You may know people who have developed problems from working too long at a computer without taking care of their health. These problems can include an aching back, neck or wrists and are commonly known as RSI (repetitive strain injury). Unfortunately, once you get such injuries, it can take years to recover and can have long-term consequences for your working life.

### 1.3.2 Avoiding Problems

Taking simple precautions can help you avoid the more severe health problems and also many computer-related accidents.

- Set up your workstation properly. Have enough room to sit and work comfortably, use an adjustable chair that is the right height and has a back support, use a wrist rest and position the top of the monitor roughly level with your eyes.

- Take regular breaks. Most RSI comes from continuous work on a keyboard or mouse when the hands and body are held stiffly in the same position for too long.

- Keep cables and bags, coats etc. off the floor so there is no danger of tripping up.
- Avoid glare. Adjust settings so that the monitor is not too bright, use blinds or turn the desk round.

## 1.4 Discovering the Desktop

### 1.4.1 GUI (Graphical User Interface)

Windows-style operating systems allow you to work intuitively with a computer. Instead of typing in instructions in code, you can select recognisable items and read from menus without needing to understand much about how the computer works. This is known as a GUI.

One advantage of a GUI is that you can see your work in different views and check how it is going to look on paper before you actually print it out. This facility is referred to as WYSIWYG (what you see is what you get).

### 1.4.2 The Desktop

When you start working on a computer, your opening screen – referred to as the desktop – will display a number of items:

**1** *Icons* – these are pictures representing parts of the computer such as the computer itself (My Computer), a waste bin (the Recycle Bin) and an area to store your work (My Documents).

**2** *Bars* – at the bottom of the screen you will find the grey taskbar that contains information about the computer, and you may also have a Microsoft Office Shortcut bar providing links to various programs.

**3** *Buttons* – in the bottom left-hand corner of the screen is the **Start** button which is often the starting point for a computer session. You will also find a variety of buttons on the taskbar that you press to open up menus, programs or files.

**4** *Menus* – clicking the **Start** button, for example, opens up the **Start** menu which then offers you a further menu of programs on the computer.

**5** *Background* – to improve the enjoyment of working on a computer, you can change the appearance of your screen, including the colours and pictures that form the background to the desktop.

You will also see a pointer. Whenever you move the mouse, a pointer moves across the screen and can be positioned over any object. The pointer takes on different shapes depending on what is happening or which area of the screen it is over.

## 1.4.3 Working with Windows

When you double click any icon or launch a program, it opens into a window. You can have any number of windows open on screen at the same time, but you will always be working in just one window at a time – the *active* window. All other open windows will be behind the active window or available as buttons on the taskbar.

All windows have a similar basic structure:

**1** *Title bar* – the bar across the top of the window housing the program or file name. When a window is active, this bar is blue. When inactive, it is grey.

**2** *Menu bar* – this houses the menus that are relevant to the specific program or file, but will usually include File, Edit, View, Tools and Help.

    [A] File menu for opening, creating, saving and printing files.

    [B] Edit menu for moving, selecting or copying files.

    [C] Tools menu for links to basic settings.

    [D] View menu for ways to view the contents of the window.

    [E] Help menu for guidance on how to carry out particular tasks.

**3** *Toolbar* – one or more bars holding shortcuts to common tasks. If any are missing, right click any toolbar and select another from the list that will appear.

**4** *Scroll bars* – click the arrows or drag the grey box to move up or down the window or from left to right.

**5** *Tasks pane* – this is an extra pane that may be visible at some times or can be added from the **View** menu. It offers shortcuts to a variety of tasks, depending on which activity you are trying to carry out.

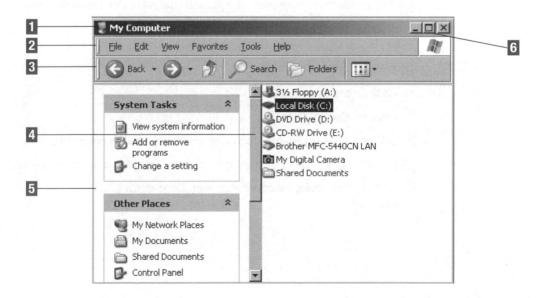

**6** *Control buttons* – all windows can be controlled by clicking one of these buttons.

  **A** Close: closes the window.

  **B** Minimise: reduces the window to a button on the taskbar.

  **C** Maximise: expands the window to fill the entire screen.

  **D** Restore down: this alternates with Maximise. Click this button to restore the window to its previous size.

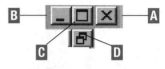

## 1.5 Basic Settings

### 1.5.1 Settings that can be Changed

If things go wrong, for example if the date is incorrect, if you cannot hear your CDs or if the screen icons are too small, you can usually change the settings. Common changes you might want to make:

1 *Sounds and Audio Devices* – lets you mute or allow sounds and set the noise levels.

2 *Regional and Language Options* – lets you check that dates and currency are correct for the UK or a specific country.

3 *Display* – has settings for the background, animated screen savers, resolution of the screen and monitor colours.

4 *Keyboard* – has settings for the character repeat speed.

5 *Date and Time* – allows you to click on a calendar, select a different month and day or click arrows to move to a different time.

6 *Add* or *Remove Programs* – the place to get rid of unwanted software.

7 *Mouse* – lets you slow down the double click speed.

### 1.5.2 Changing Basic Settings

1 *Click on the Start button.*

2 *Click on Control Panel.*

3 *Double click to open the icon or item name to view its properties.*

4 *For Display, you can also right click on the desktop and select Properties.*

5 *Change any settings that are incorrect. Drop-down arrows or checkboxes will be available.*

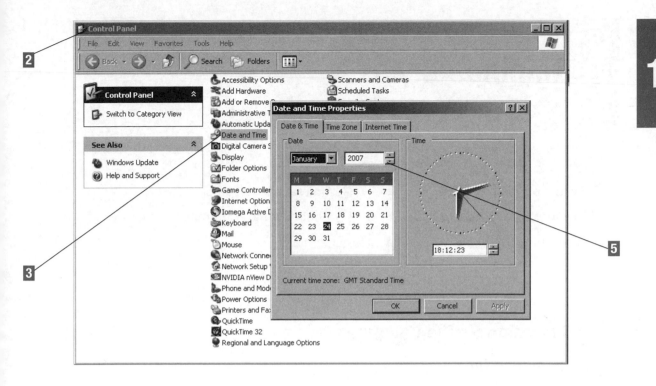

# CHAPTER 2

# Gaining Access

## What You'll Do

→ Switch on the computer

→ Use login procedures

→ Restart the computer

→ Unfreeze a computer

→ Shut down the computer

## 2.1 Switching On the Computer

### 2.1.1 Switching On

**Assessment Objective 1a**

Starting up a computer is simply a matter of pressing the **On** switch. If nothing appears on the monitor, it probably means that this has been turned off: monitors have their own power switch.

## 2.2 Login Procedures

### 2.2.1 Why You Log In

To protect your area on a network, particularly if you are storing sensitive files, financial information or personal details, you will need to identify yourself to the computer each time you start work. This is known as logging in (or on) and involves entering two identifiers – your ID or username and a password. You usually set up these details when you first register somewhere like a college, on a website or with an Internet Service Provider.

The ID is often an email address or your name combined with a department, staff or course number. In many organisations it takes on a standard format and so is probably known to a large number of people.

The password is a combination of letters and numbers chosen by you that nobody else should know. When you type it in, only **** or • • • • will be visible on screen, so that no-one can read the details over your shoulder.

The combination of ID and password is required to allow you to access your personal workspace.

When logging in, you may also have to select the department or establishment in which you work.

## 2.2.2 Logging In

**1** *Type your ID in the Username box.*

**2** *Type your password in the Password box.*

**3** *Select your authorised working area if required from the list in the Log on to: box.*

**4** *Click Options if you want to change your password.*

**5** *Click OK to start work.*

**6** *At the end of a computer session, always log off.*

**Log On to Windows**

Microsoft
**Windows** xp
Professional

Copyright © 1985-2001
Microsoft Corporation

*Microsoft*

**1** ──────── User name:

**2** ──────── Password:

**3** ──────── Log on to:

OK    Cancel    Shut Down...    Options <<  ──── **4**

## 2.2.3 Passwords

To make sure your password is safe:

- Choose one that won't be easy to guess. Ideally it should combine upper and lower case letters, numbers and accepted punctuation symbols.

- Change the password regularly.

- Never write it down or tell other people what it is.

**My password isn't accepted!**

Take care when entering your password to type it exactly, as passwords are normally *case sensitive*.

## 2.3 | Restarting the Computer

During a computer session, you may need to turn off the computer but want to continue working. A common reason is when you install new software as some of your start up files will need to be re-written. If you restart you do not completely turn off the machine but still allow it to reset files and settings.

### 2.3.1 Restarting a Computer

1. *Click on the Start Button.*

2. *Click Turn Off Computer.*

3. *Click the Restart button in the Turn off computer window.*

You could also try holding down the **Ctrl** and **Alt** keys and pressing **Delete** twice.

Turn off computer

Stand By    Turn Off    Restart

Cancel

### 2.3.2 Unfreezing a Computer

If the mouse or a window suddenly stops responding, you may be able to get the computer working again by closing that particular program.

1. *Right click the taskbar.*

2. *Click Task Manager.*

3. *Click the program showing in the window that is not running.*

4. *Click End Task.*

You can also call up the Task Manager by holding down **Ctrl** and **Alt** and pressing **Delete**.

## 2.4 | Shutting Down

### 2.4.1 Shutting Down a Computer

As you work, temporary files will be created and your current work will not necessarily have been saved correctly. You should therefore never simply press the power switch off. Instead, follow a proper shut down procedure.

1. *Click the Start button.*

2. *Click Turn Off Computer.*

3. *Click the Turn Off button showing in the window.*

# CHAPTER 3

# Getting Started with Word

## What You'll Do

→ Discover Word

→ Create a document

→ Save a document

→ Open an existing document

→ Print a document

## 3.1 Word

**3**

### 3.1.1 What is Word?

Word is a powerful word processing application that will enable you to produce a wide range of documents incorporating text, images, charts or tables. The text can be formatted and laid out in different ways and you will find many useful facilities to help you work with long documents.

### 3.1.2 Launching Word

1 *Click on the Start button.*

2 *Click on All Programs.*

3 *Click on Microsoft Word.*

If you have a shortcut to Word on the Start menu or Office Shortcut bar, click that instead.

## 3.1.3 The Word screen

When the program opens, you will see a blank document in the centre of the screen.

The Word window has the following components:

**1** *Cursor* is a black flashing bar marking the position for text insertion.

**2** *Standard toolbar* offers shortcuts to tasks such as creating documents, opening existing documents, saving and printing.

**3** *Formatting toolbar* provides a quick way to change the look of your text or paragraphs.

**4** *Drawing toolbar* offers tools for adding shapes and images to the document.

**5** *Task pane* is an extra pane that appears on the right hand side of the screen whenever certain tasks are carried out. You can click the close button at the top of the pane to remove it if you prefer an uncluttered screen.

**6** *Status bar* across the bottom of the document displays details about the document such as page numbers and the position of the cursor.

**7** *Rulers* are available in some views to help position objects.

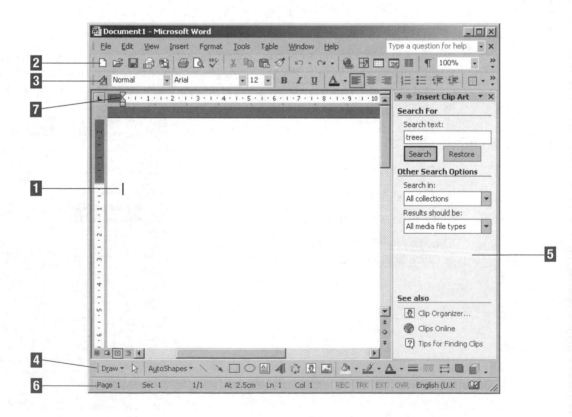

## 3.1.4　Different Views

You can view your screen in a variety of ways:

**1** *Normal* is the default view for entering and editing text.

**2** *Web Layout* displays the page as it would appear on the World Wide Web.

**3** *Print Layout* allows you to work with pictures and drawings and shows what the document will look like when printed.

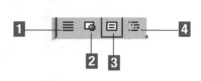

**4** *Outline* enables you to work on the structure of a long document.

To change view:

⌐1⌐ *Click the View menu.*

⌐2⌐ *Click the preferred view.*

Or

⌐3⌐ *Click one of the View buttons visible in the bottom, left hand corner of the screen.*

## 3.2　Creating Documents

### 3.2.1　Creating a Document

**Assessment Objective 1b**

Every time you open Word, a blank document titled Document1 is ready for you to type into. To create a document:

⌐1⌐ *Click the File menu.*

⌐2⌐ Click New.

**3** *In the Task pane that will open, click Blank Document.*

Or

**4** *Click the New button on the standard toolbar.*

A keyboard shortcut is **Ctrl–N**.

Subsequent documents will be titled Document2, 3, 4 etc. until you save and name them.

## 3.2.2 Using Templates

Instead of starting with a blank document, you can make use of professionally styled documents stored as templates. When you customise a template to create your own document, the original will remain unchanged.

1. *Click the File menu.*

2. *Click New.*

3. *In the Task pane, click General Templates.*

4. *Select a style of document such as a letter, fax or report.*

5. *View it in Preview.*

6. *Check that Create New Document is selected.*

7. *Click OK.*

## 3.3 Saving

### 3.3.1 Saving a Document for the First Time

**Assessment Objective 1d**

It is very important to save documents systematically, so that you can find them again easily. You need to decide:

■ What name to give the document.

■ Where to store it.

At any stage you can save the document on your computer.

1 *Click the File menu.*

2 *Click Save.*

Or

3 *Click the Save button on the standard toolbar.*

4 *If the correct location is not showing in the Save in: box, click the down facing arrow to display a list of alternative locations.*

5 *You can also click a location on the Places bar.*

Or

6 *Click the Up arrow to search for a different location.*

7 *Accept or edit the name showing in the File name: box.*

8 *Click the Save button or press Enter.*

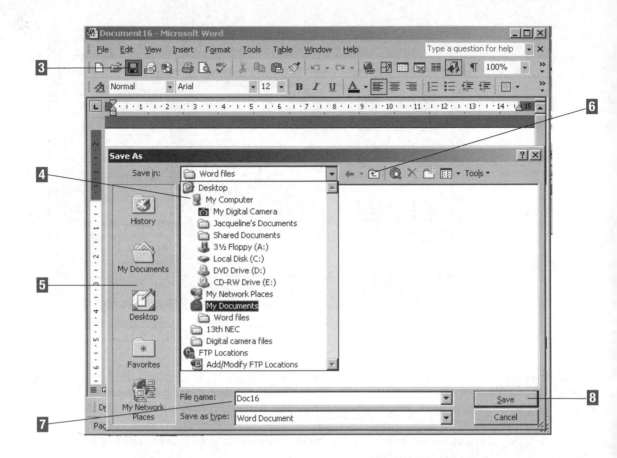

## Does the file name matter?

When taking an assessment, make sure that you give your document the specified file name and that this does not contain any errors. It may be displayed on your printouts.

## Save regularly

Keep documents safe. Click the Save button regularly to make sure you update your work and keep the latest changes. A keyboard shortcut is **Ctrl–S**.

## 3.3.2 Using Save As

When you want to keep a copy of a document as backup, or create a different version, you can save a second copy with a different name and/or to a different location.

1. *Click the File menu.*

2. *Click Save As.*

3. *Edit the file name that will appear in the File name: box.*

4 *Keep the same location or select a different one.*

5 *Click Save.*

## When should I use Save As?

Make sure you use it early or you may click Save by mistake and overwrite your original document with later changes.

## 3.4 Opening Documents

### 3.4.1 Opening an Existing Document

**Assessment Objective 1c**

Having saved your documents with meaningful names, you will be able to locate and open them again easily. For New CLAIT, you will be provided with a document you must locate and open.

1 *Click the File menu.*

2 *Click Open.*

Or

3 *Click the Open toolbar button on the standard toolbar* 📂.

4 *Search for the location of the document so that it appears in the Look in: box.*

5 *Click the name of the document showing in the window.*

6 *Click Open or press Enter.*

**3**

4 ——

| Open | ? ✕ |

Look in: 📁 Word files

📄 Boats  📄 Business reports  📄 **Habitats**  📄 Letter to Stirling fabrics  📄 Pet Centre details  📄 Sports fixtures —— 5

📄 Waste disposal

History
My Documents
Desktop
Favorites
My Network Places

File name:  [ ]  Open —— 6
Files of type: All Files  Cancel

### 3.4.2 Moving Between Open Documents

Once you have a number of documents open, you can switch between them in different ways:

- Open the Window menu and click the name of the document you want to work with.

- Click the name of the document showing as a button on the taskbar.

- Hold down **Alt** and keep clicking the **Tab** key until the document you want to open is selected. When you let go of the mouse the selected file will open on screen.

## 3.5 Printing

### 3.5.1 Printers

**Assessment Objective 1e**

Depending on the way your computer is set up, it may be linked to one or more printers. One of these will be the default printer: using a shortcut to print your documents will automatically send them to this one.

All printers are different, but they all have one or more paper trays or feeds for loading the paper. Commercial printers often have touch screen menus for selecting different types of paper or methods for collating and stapling long documents.

When printing, only change settings in the Print box if you want to print something other than a single copy of the entire document.

**Critical Error**
Any missing printouts.

### 3.5.2 Printing a Document

1. *Click the File menu.*

2. *Click Print.*

3. *When the Print box opens, click in the Current page button to print only the page open on screen.*

4. *Click Pages and enter page numbers or a range of numbers to print selected parts of the document.*

5. *Click the arrow in the Printer Name box if you want to select a different printer.*

6. *Click in the Number of copies: box and use the up or down arrows or enter an exact figure to print more than one copy.*

7. *When all settings are correct, click OK or press Enter.*

**Print** dialog box showing:

- Printer section: Name: Brother MFC-5440CN Printer, Properties, Find Printer..., Print to file, Manual duplex. Status: Idle, Type: Brother MFC-5440CN Printer, Where: BRN_731FB1, Comment: BRN_731FB1
- Page range: All, Current page, Selection, Pages. "Enter page numbers and/or page ranges separated by commas. For example, 1,3,5–12"
- Copies: Number of copies, Collate
- Print what: Document, Print: All pages in range
- Zoom: Pages per sheet: 1 page, Scale to paper size: No Scaling
- Options..., OK, Cancel

**5**, **3**, **4**, **6**

For a copy of the entire document using the default settings, click the Print toolbar button or use the keyboard shortcut **Ctrl–P**.

## 3.5.3  Taking a Screen Print

The New CLAIT assessment will ask you to print images of the screen showing icons or windows, as well as actual documents. To do this you need to take a screen print. This image is then copied into a word processed document.

1. *With the required items displayed on screen, press the Print Screen (Prt Scr) button at the top of the keyboard.*

2. *Hold **Alt** as you press the key to take a picture of the active window only.*

3. *Open a word processed document.*

4. *Click the Edit menu or right click.*

5. *Click Copy.*

6. *Type any text and name, save or print the document as normal.*

### Check the screen print

Every item that should be visible on the screen print must be clearly displayed or you will be marked down.

## 3.6 Closing

### 3.6.1 Closing a Document

1. *Click the lower Close button in the top, right hand corner.*

Or

2. *Click the File menu.*

3. *Click Close.*

## 3.7 Exiting

### 3.7.1 Exiting Word

1. *Click the upper Close button at the top of the screen.*

Or

2. *Click the File menu.*

3. *Click Exit.*

# CHAPTER 4

# Folders and Files

## What You'll Do

➔ Discover files, folders and applications

➔ Search for folders and files

➔ Create and name a folder

➔ Rename a file or folder

➔ Delete a file or folder

➔ Move files

➔ Copy files

## 4.1 | Files, Folders and Applications

### 4.1.1 What is the Difference?

You will find the following items on your computer that you must be able to recognise.

*Files* are individually stored items of information such as word processed documents or web pages. They are named and will have a specific format. The application with which they are associated will be shown by a small icon.

- costing
- SAND 2007
- Booking Chart 2007
- old goal
- Managing the engine

Files produced when working with different applications have a generic name, for example:

Word files are referred to as *documents*.

Excel files are referred to as *workbooks* (or *spreadsheets*).

Access files are referred to as *databases*.

FrontPage files are referred to as *web pages*.

PowerPoint files are referred to as *presentations*.

*Programs* are complex collections of files installed on your computer that help you carry out specific tasks. You may find them pre-installed, or you can install them from a CD-ROM or after downloading from the Internet. The main part of the program will be an executable file, but associated files may include guides to the program, image or sound files and licence documents.

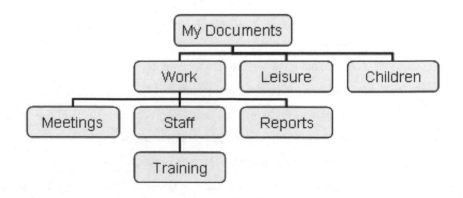

| Name ▲ | Type | Date Modified |
|---|---|---|
| html | File Folder | 05/07/2003 19:57 |
| Air | MIDI Sequence | 10/11/2001 23:52 |
| anvctrls.ocx | ActiveX Control | 20/02/2000 11:23 |
| AnvilFlt.OCX | ActiveX Control | 02/06/2001 11:10 |
| astudio | Application | 26/06/2003 17:42 |
| asUpgr | Application | 28/04/2002 02:07 |
| Autoplay.ply | PLY File | 11/11/2001 08:07 |
| FugueGM | MIDI Sequence | 10/11/2001 23:49 |
| LoopDemo | MIDI Sequence | 22/06/2002 14:03 |
| Loopo_a | Wave Sound | 21/09/2001 15:57 |
| Loopo_b | Wave Sound | 21/09/2001 16:07 |
| MidiCtl.ocx | ActiveX Control | 21/05/2003 16:19 |
| Sonata-c | MIDI Sequence | 10/11/2001 23:52 |
| ST5UNST | Text Document | 05/07/2003 19:58 |

*Folders* are areas set aside for storing related groups of files and are sometimes referred to as directories. They always appear in Windows XP computers as named yellow boxes.

## 4.1.2 Organisation of Folders

Folders are organised in a hierarchy and can be visualised as a large family tree. Those at the top can hold an increasing number of folders as you can continually subdivide your folders into subfolders.

**Folders structure**

## 4.1.3 Viewing Files and Folders

When working with files, folders or programs on the desktop, you can view them in different ways by changing options on the menu.

1. *Open My Documents or My Computer*.

2. *Double click any folder to view its contents*.

3. *Click the View menu*.

Or

4. *Click the drop down arrow next to the Views button*.

5. *Click to select one of the options, which will then show a large black dot next to its name*:

- A *Thumbnails* to see icons and small pictures of any image files.

- B *Tiles* to see them as large icons with details of their size and file type.

- C *Icons* to see smaller versions showing just the file name.

- D *List* to see a simple list of file names.

- E *Details* to see information about the file size, type, date it was created etc.

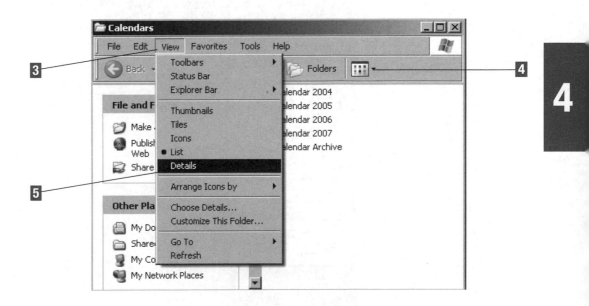

## 4.2 Searching

However carefully you store files or programs, it is common to misplace them now and again. Use the Windows search facilities to locate a folder or file.

### 4.2.1 Using Search

[1] *Click the Start button.*

[2] *Click Search.*

Or

[3] *Click the Search button on any window open on the desktop.*

[4] *Within each application, there may also be a Search option available from the drop down list in the Tasks pane.*

[5] *In the Search Results box, click the appropriate type of search. If you don't know what type of item you are looking for, select All files and folders.*

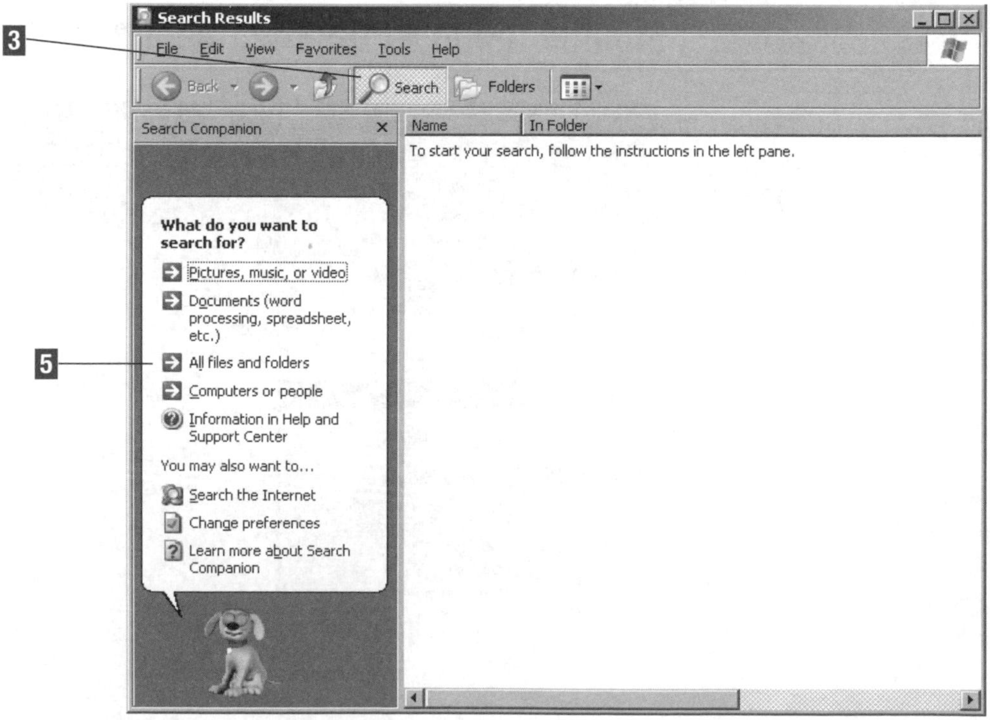

6. *Type as much of the file or folder name as you know into the name box.*

7. *Click the drop down arrow in the Look in: box and select the most likely drive or folder location. To select a specific location on your computer, first click Browse.*

8. *Click one of the advanced options to specify when the file was modified or its size, if this will speed up the search.*

9. *Click the Search button.*

10. *Files and folders containing the specified name will be displayed in the main window.*

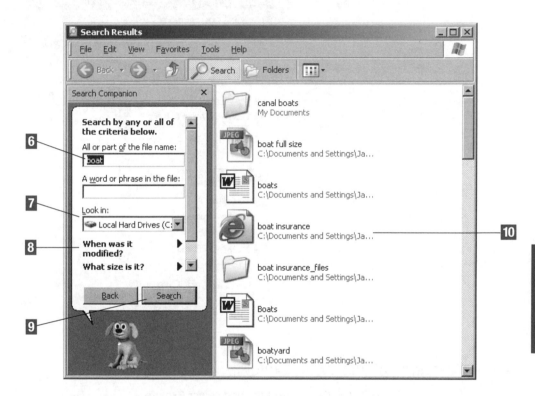

## 4.3 Creating Folders

### 4.3.1 Creating and Naming a Folder

**Assessment Objective 2a**

Once you have saved a number of files on a related theme, you can group them together in a folder so that they are easy to locate. You can create folders on the desktop using the Windows File and Folder Tasks pane or you can open a special file management program named Explorer.

## 4.3.2  Creating Folders Using the Tasks Pane

**1** *Open My Documents or the parent folder.*

**2** *Click **Make a new folder** in the File and Folder Tasks pane.*

**3** *When the new folder appears, type its name over the highlighted text.*

**4** *Press Enter or click the mouse to complete the naming.*

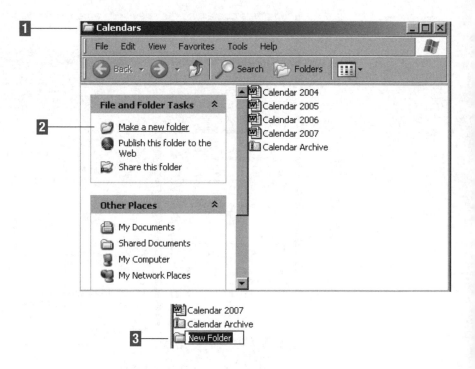

## 4.3.3  Creating Folders Using Explorer

**1** *Right click the Start button and select Explore.*

Or

**2** *Click the Folders button in My Documents or an open folder. This reveals the folders structure of your computer.*

**3** *Scroll down the left pane if necessary until you can see the parent folder.*

**4** *If you know it is inside another folder, you may need to click a + sign to display the contents.*

**5** *Click the folder name.*

**6** *Click the File menu.*

**7** *Click New Folder.*

8  *Type in the name when the folder appears.*

9  *If you open the parent folder, you can also use the following method:*

   A  *Click to open the File menu.*

   B  *Click New.*

   C  *Click New Folder.*

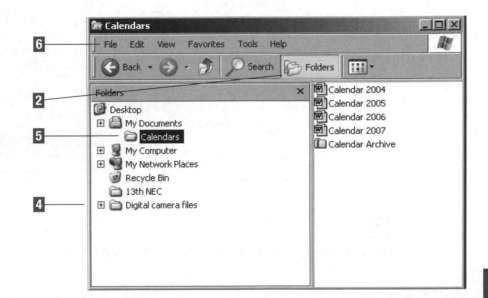

## 4.4  Renaming

### 4.4.1  Renaming a File or Folder

**Assessment Objective 2b**

1  *Select the file or folder.*

2  *Click Rename this file in the Tasks pane.*

Or

3  *Right click the file or folder name.*

4  *Click Rename on the menu that will appear.*

Or

5  *Click once on a file or folder name.*

6  *Click in the name box to edit the name, or replace it completely by typing directly into the box.*

7  *Click the mouse to complete the naming.*

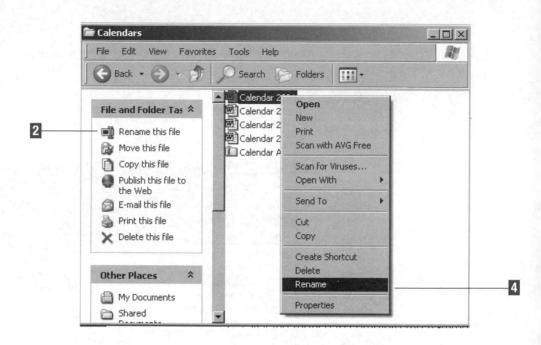

---

## Take care when naming

When taking an assessment, check that you have named your folders accurately.

# 4.5 Deleting

## 4.5.1 Deleting a File or Folder

**Assessment Objective 2c**

It is very simple to delete an unwanted file or folder. Select it and then:

1. *Press the Delete key.*

Or

2. *Click the Delete option in the Tasks pane.*

Or

3. *Right click and select Delete from the menu.*

## What if I delete a file or folder by mistake?

It will not have been removed completely but will have been transferred to the Recycle Bin. Open this and select the Restore option to return the file or folder to its original location.

**I've deleted some important files!**

Take care to remove the contents of a folder before deleting if it contains any files you want to keep. Otherwise the folder and all its contents will be deleted at the same time.

**Critical Error**
Failure to delete a specified file or folder.

## 4.6 Moving Files

### 4.6.1 Different Methods

**Assessment Objective 2d**

Once you start organising your work into folders, you will want to move specific files into more appropriate locations. There are three methods for doing this:

- Dragging with the mouse when you can see the file and target folder on screen at the same time.

- Using a technique known as cut and paste when you need time to locate the destination folder.

- Using the Tasks pane.

**When I tried to select a file to move, it opened instead**

This can easily happen by mistake. Simply close it again to return to the desktop.

### 4.6.2 Moving by Dragging

1. *Open My Documents.*

2. *Open the folder containing the file you want to move.*

3. *If the file and destination folder are both visible in the same window, you will be able to drag the file straight into the folder.*

4. *If they are not, click the Folders button to use Explorer.*

5. *Click the file when the pointer shows a left facing white arrow.*

6. *Keep holding down the mouse button as you drag the file towards the destination folder.*

7. *Let go when the folder turns blue.*

### What do I do if I move a file into the wrong folder?

If you have already done this, open the folder and move it out again. To prevent this happening in future, drag the file with the right mouse button. When you let go you will display a menu offering the option of moving or copying the file or cancelling the action.

## 4.6.3 Moving a Number of Files at the Same Time

1. *Select a range of files: click the first and then hold* **Shift** *as you click the last. All files in the range will be selected.*

2. *Select individual files: click the first and then hold* **Ctrl** *as you click other file names. They will all stay selected.*

3. *Drag one and they will all be moved at the same time.*

## 4.6.4 Moving Using Cut and Paste

1. *Display the file you want to move.*

2. *Right click the file.*

3. *Click Cut.*

Or

4. *Select the file, open the Edit menu and click Cut.*

5. *The file icon will become paler.*

6. *Open the destination folder. You may need to click the Up arrow to work up through your folders.*

7. *Click Paste – available in the same way as Cut.*

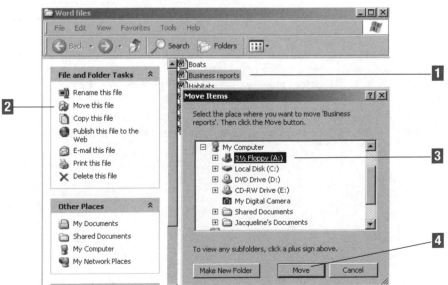

You could also use the keyboard shortcuts for Cut (**Ctrl–X**) and Paste (**Ctrl–V**.)

## 4.6.5 Moving Using the Tasks Pane

**1** *Click the file you want to move.*

**2** *Click **Move this file** in the Tasks pane. (This option is also available from the Edit menu.)*

**3** *Click a destination folder in the window that will open.*

**4** *Click Move.*

## 4.7 Copying Files

### 4.7.1 Making Copies

Being able to place a copy of a file in a different location is very useful when you want to take it away from the computer on removable storage media, or if you want to keep a backup by saving the same file in two different folders on your computer.

### 4.7.2 Copying by Dragging

1. *Open My Documents.*

2. *Open the folder containing the file you want to copy.*

3. *Click the file when the pointer shows a left facing white arrow and keep holding down the mouse button.*

4. *Hold down the **Ctrl** key. This will add a + sign in a box to the pointer arrow.*

5. *Drag the file towards the destination folder.*

6. *Let go of the mouse and then the key when the folder turns blue.*

Or

7. *Drag using the right mouse button.*

8. *When you let go, select Copy Here from the menu that will appear.*

### 4.7.3 Copying Using Copy and Paste

1. *Display the file you want to copy.*

2. *Right click the file.*

3. *Click Copy.*

Or

4. *Select the file, open the Edit menu and click Copy.*

5. *Open the destination folder.*

6. *Click Paste – available in the same way as Copy.*

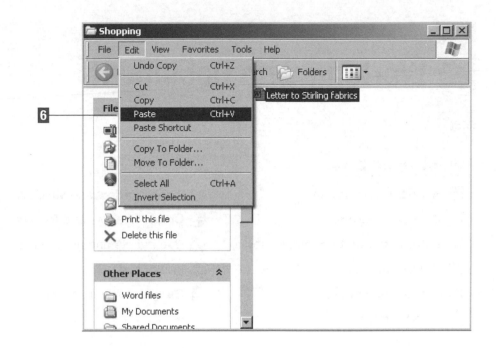

You could also click the file and use the keyboard shortcut for Copy: **Ctrl–C**.

## 4.7.4 Copying Using the Tasks Pane

1. *Click the file you want to copy.*

2. *Click Copy this file in the Tasks pane. (This option is also available from the Edit menu.)*

3. *Click a destination folder in the window that will open.*

4. *Click Copy.*

# CHAPTER 5

# Working with Documents

## What You'll Do

→ Set page orientation

→ Set page margins

→ Enter text, numbers and symbols

→ Correct mistakes

→ Set text alignment

→ Insert a table

→ Apply borders and shading

→ Create headers and footers

→ Use bullets and numbering

→ Indent text

→ Carry out a word count

## 5.1 Page Layout

### 5.1.1 Default Layouts

Every document has the basic settings – known as the default – applied automatically. This means that you can open Word and create a document very quickly, without having to set up the page before you start.

Default settings include the width of the margins round the edge of the page; the size and appearance of the text; the way the document will print out; and how the text lines up on the page. All these can be changed to suit your particular preferences.

### 5.1.2 Changing Page Orientation

**Assessment Objective 3a**

Documents such as letters, invoices or leaflets are usually needed in *portrait* orientation, so that they print on paper that has sides longer than the width. On A4 paper, for example, this means printouts that are 21 cm wide and 29.7 cm in height.

If you want a page printed with the longer sides top and bottom you need to change to *landscape* orientation.

1. *Click the File menu.*

2. *Click Page Setup.*

3. *Click Margins if it is not the uppermost tab.*

**4** *Click the correct orientation button.*

**5** *Click OK.*

## 5.1.3  Changing Page Margins

White space is left round the edge of the paper when documents are printed. These are the margins. Default settings are:

   Top and bottom margins 2.54 cm.

   Left and right margins 3.17 cm.

To increase or decrease any of these measurements for particular documents:

[1] *Click the File menu.*

[2] *Click Page Setup.*

[3] *Click the Margins tab if it is not uppermost.*

**4** *Click in one of the margin boxes and type your own measurement.*

Or

[5] *Click the up or down arrows to change the measurement in steps of 1/10th cm.*

**6** *Click OK to confirm the new setting and close the Page Setup box.*

**How can I increase a margin by 1/100th cm?**

You will need to type in the exact measure in the box as the arrows will not increase units by such small amounts.

**My margin doesn't look right**

If asked to *increase* a margin by a set amount, you must add this to the measure in the box, not set this as the margin measurement.

**What is the allowable error?**

For an assessment, you are allowed only a 3 mm tolerance for each margin.

## 5.2 Text, Numbers and Symbols

### 5.2.1 Creating Documents

Creating a document involves typing in letters, numbers or punctuation symbols. If you have previously used a typewriter, you will find it very similar. The flashing cursor on screen will show the position where your text will appear.

Conventions differ, but you usually leave one space between words and one or two spaces at the end of each sentence.

When taking an assessment, aim to use the same case as that shown in the assignment.

## 5.2.2 Entering Characters

**Assessment Objective 3d**

1. *Press any letter key to type a lower case letter.*

2. *Press any number key for a number. You can use the number pad on the right of most keyboards, or the main row of numbers.*

3. *Press a key for a punctuation symbol displayed at the bottom such as = , / or #.*

4. *Hold **Shift** as you press a key for a capital letter or upper punctuation symbol such as @ ? + or ^.*

5. *Press the **Caps Lock** key if you want to type a long entry in capitals. Press it again to return to normal typing.*

6. *Press the **Space bar** to add a space between characters or words.*

### What can I do if I find I have typed all my text in capital letters by mistake?

Select the text you want to change, hold **Shift** and press the function key labelled **F3** at the top of the keyboard. Keep pressing **F3** until your text looks correct.

### I suddenly lost my work and found I was on a new page!

Take care with capitals: if you hold **Ctrl** rather than **Shift** you will use a shortcut to common tasks such as saving (**Ctrl–S**), printing (**Ctrl–P**) or opening a new document (**Ctrl–N**). If this happens, close the box or window to return to your document.

## 5.2.3 Word Wrap

One difference between word processors and typewriters is that you do not take any action when your last word reaches the end of the line. Keep typing and the application will move the word onto the next line automatically. This process is known as word wrap.

To deliberately start on a new line, press Enter. To create a new paragraph separated by a clear line space, press Enter twice.

### I have split my paragraph

Take care not to press Enter when there is text to the right of the cursor. This will be moved down the page at the same time.

**My document doesn't match the text I am copying exactly**

Your text is not expected to match line by line, so make sure that you use word wrap. If you press Enter at the end of each line (so that they end with a particular word, for example), future formatting will not be applied correctly.

## 5.2.4 Moving Round a Document

To work on one part of a document, you have several choices as to how to move the cursor into position.

1. *Click on screen with the mouse when the pointer displays a vertical bar.*

2. *To move below text already typed, double click the pointer to position the cursor or press the Enter key at the end of the last line.*

3. *Press an arrow (cursor) key in the appropriate direction.*

4. *Click an arrow or drag the grey box in the scroll bar to move up or down the page.*

Or

5. *Press the **Page Up** or **Page Down** keys.*

6. *Press **Home** to move to the start of the line.*

7. *Hold **Ctrl** and press **Home** to move to the start of the entire text.*

8. *Press **End** to move to the end of the line.*

9. *Hold **Ctrl** and press **End** to move to the end of the entire text.*

## 5.3 Checking Documents

### 5.3.1 Why Bother?

As well as losing marks in an assignment, no-one wants to create documents that contain inaccuracies, and so you need to use all the available facilities to correct any mistakes before your work is printed or circulated. However, never rely on the computer completely.

### 5.3.2 Proof Reading

Read through your text very carefully on screen and correct any errors. These may creep in because of transposed characters (*was* for *saw*), a slip of the finger (*teal* for *teak*), text left unfinished or copied incorrectly, or inaccurate information that cannot be picked up by the spelling or grammar checkers built into Word.

A common mistake is the wrong spacing for hyphenated words or using an en dash. There should be no space before or after a hyphen:

X-ray is correct

X –ray, X- ray and X – ray are incorrect.

### 5.3.3  The Spell Checker

When you type a word that is not in the computer's built-in dictionary, a red wavy line will appear underneath it. You can change the word, leave it as it is or add it to the dictionary so that it is not picked up in future. In this way, you can build up a personal dictionary of proper names and specialist words that are unlikely to be included in the standard list.

### 5.3.4  The Grammar Checker

You will see green wavy lines under:

- Incorrect spacing. Leave one space after commas and one or two after full stops.

- Fragments. You may have ended headings or subheadings with a full stop so that the computer expects them to be complete sentences.

- Sentences not agreeing with in-built rules of grammar such as single nouns with plural verbs.

**Danger – grammar checker at work!**

If you select an alternative grammar correction, this often changes the actual wording of your text. In New CLAIT the words must match the assessment piece exactly. This also applies to the spacing in the original document if you edit one supplied.

⊗ **Critical Error**
**Making unrequested amendments to the text in a text file with which you are provided.**

### 5.3.5  Checking One Word or Phrase

1. *Right click the red or green underlined words.*

2. *Click the correct replacement if it is offered.*

3. *Click Ignore to leave it unchanged.*

4. *Click Add to Dictionary if it is spelt correctly and you expect to use it again.*

5. *Click AutoCorrect if you often type it by mistake. You can select an alternative that will replace it automatically.*

6. *Click Spelling (or Grammar) to open the Spelling and Grammar box.*

**5**

## 5.3.6  Checking a Document

**1** *Click the Spelling and Grammar toolbar button.*

**2** *Click an alternative word in the Suggestions box.*

**3** *If a suitable alternative is not offered, click into the incorrect word and change it manually.*

**4** *Click a Change option to update the document.*

    **A** *Change to change the single occurrence.*

    **B** *Change All to change the word throughout the document.*

**5** *Click an Ignore option to leave it in place.*

**6** *Click Cancel to leave the spelling and grammar box.*

## Spelling and Grammar: English (U.K.) dialog

**Not in Dictionary:**

In this case we **mus** not be

Buttons: Ignore Once, Ignore All, Add to Dictionary

**Suggestions:**

muss
must
musk
muse
mush
mums

Buttons: Change, Change All, AutoCorrect

**Dictionary language:** English (U.K.)

☑ Check grammar

Buttons: Options..., Undo, Cancel

Callout numbers: 3, 2, 5, 4, 6

## 5.3.7 Using Undo

It is easy to make silly mistakes such as deleting the wrong text or moving text to the wrong place. Take quick action to put things right.

**1** *Click the Undo button to step back through your actions.*

**2** *Click the drop down arrow next to the button to select and undo a number of actions in one go.*

**3** *Click the Redo button if you step back too far.*

Or

**4** *Click to open the Edit menu.*

**5** *Click the appropriate undo or redo option.*

Undo button

# 5.4 Text Alignment

## 5.4.1 Types of Alignment

Assessment Objective 3c

As you type, text will normally line up on the left margin. This is known as left alignment. You can change the setting for any line. The choices are:

**1** Left alignment – normal typing with text lined up on the left margin.

**2** Central alignment – text spreads from a central point on the page.

**3** Right alignment – text lines up on the right margin.

**4** Justified – spaces are added to straighten both edges. This is a common text alignment for large blocks of text.

5

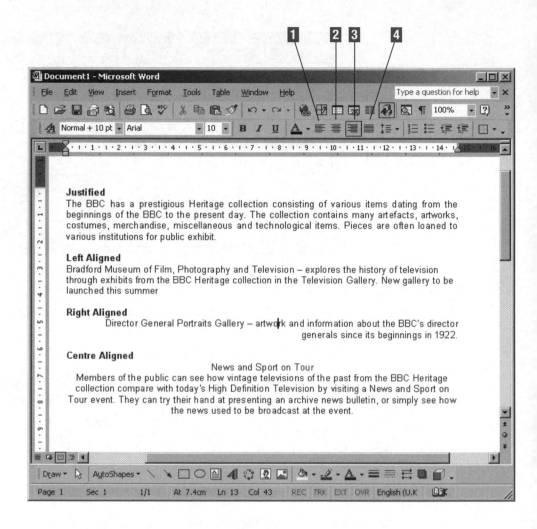

**Justified**

The BBC has a prestigious Heritage collection consisting of various items dating from the beginnings of the BBC to the present day. The collection contains many artefacts, artworks, costumes, merchandise, miscellaneous and technological items. Pieces are often loaned to various institutions for public exhibit.

**Left Aligned**

Bradford Museum of Film, Photography and Television – explores the history of television through exhibits from the BBC Heritage collection in the Television Gallery. New gallery to be launched this summer

**Right Aligned**

Director General Portraits Gallery – artwork and information about the BBC's director generals since its beginnings in 1922.

**Centre Aligned**

News and Sport on Tour
Members of the public can see how vintage televisions of the past from the BBC Heritage collection compare with today's High Definition Television by visiting a News and Sport on Tour event. They can try their hand at presenting an archive news bulletin, or simply see how the news used to be broadcast at the event.

---

**Can I have two different alignments on the same line?**

Alignment affects lines, so you cannot have mixed alignments within a single line. Move to a new line to set a different alignment.

## 5.4.2 Setting Alignment

1. *Click anywhere on the line to select a single paragraph or click and drag to select a block of text extending over several paragraphs.*

2. *Click the appropriate alignment toolbar button.*

Or

3. *Click the Format menu.*

④ *Click Paragraph.*

⑤ *Click the drop down arrow in the Alignment box.*

⑥ *Click the chosen alignment.*

⑦ *Click OK.*

⑧ *Keep typing and the sentence or paragraph will retain the alignment.*

## 5.5 Tables

### 5.5.1 Using Tables

Assessment
Objective 3e
You can add a table to a Word document that will display data in grid format. Remove the borders to display the table contents as neat columns, or colour or thicken borders to make the table stand out.

Each square of a table is referred to as a cell. Cells are independent, so that you can change the appearance of a single cell, row or column without changing the rest of the table.

## 5.5.2 Inserting a Table

1. *Click where you want the table to appear.*

2. *Click the Insert Table toolbar button.*

3. *Click and drag the mouse across the cells to set the number of rows and columns.*

4. *Let go of the mouse and the table will appear on the page.*

Or

5. *Click the Table menu.*

6. *Click Insert.*

7. *Click Table.*

8. *Enter a measure for the number of rows and columns into the boxes.*

9. *Click OK.*

10. *Take care not to extend your table into the margins.*

11. *Click into any cell to type an entry.*

12. *Move from cell to cell by clicking the mouse or pressing the Tab key.*

### 5.5.3 Selecting Parts of a Table

Move the pointer over the table to select any part:

1. *Use the black right facing arrow to select one cell.*

2. *Use the white right facing arrow to select a row.*

3. *Use the down facing black arrow to select a column.*

4. *Click the box in the top, left hand corner showing four arrows to select the entire table.*

### 5.5.4 Formatting a Table

1. *Select the target cell(s).*

2. *Apply emphasis, alignment or a different font or font size to the cell contents by using the toolbar buttons on the formatting toolbar.*

Or

3. *Open the Format menu and change settings in the Font or Paragraph boxes.*

### 5.5.5 Editing a Table

Select any part of the table and then:

1. *Click the Table menu.*

2. *Click Insert to insert extra columns or rows.*

Or

3. *Right click the mouse.*

4. *Select an Insert option from the menu.*

5. *A quick way to add an extra row is to click in the last cell and press the Tab key.*

To delete parts of a table:

6. *Right click and select Delete.*

Or

7. *Select Delete from the Table menu.*

To fully display table contents:

8. *Click in a cell and then drag the border further to the right. Do this within the table or on the ruler.*

Or

9. *Select Table Properties from the Table menu and set exact measures for row height or column width.*

5

## 5.6 Borders and Shading

Assessment
Objective 3f Text or tables can be emphasised by adding a dark or coloured border and/or colouring the background paragraph or table cells.

### 5.6.1 Applying Borders

1. Select the text (see Chapter 6, page **55**) or table.

2. Click the Format menu.

3. Click Borders and Shading.

Or

4. For a table, right click and select this option.

5. Click the Borders tab.

6. Click None to remove a border.

7. Click Box, Shadow etc. to add a border. Tables will also have a grid option.

8. Scroll down the Styles to pick a dotted, solid or double line style.

9. Click the drop down arrow in the Color box to colour the line.

10. Click in the Width: box to increase or decrease line thickness.

11. Click in Apply to: and select the option to border just the text or single cell or the whole paragraph or table.

12. Click OK.

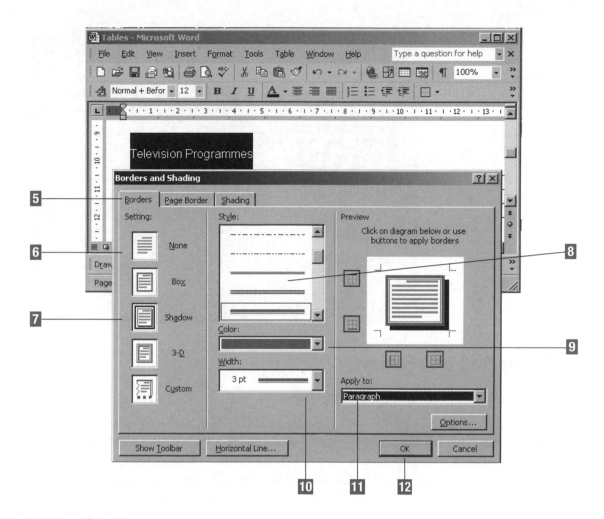

## 5.6.2  Adding Shading

1. *Click the Format menu.*

2. *Click Borders and Shading.*

3. *Click the Shading tab.*

4. *Click No Fill to remove shading.*

5. *Click a square to select the colour.*

6. *Click More Colors for a wider palette.*

7. *Click in Apply to: to shade text, paragraph, cell or whole table.*

8. *Click OK.*

5

## 5.7 | Headers and Footers

### 5.7.1  What are Headers and Footers?

**Assessment Objective 3g**

Once you have created a document, you may want to add information without changing its layout. Do this by adding entries at the top (header) or bottom (footer) of the page in the margins.

For an assignment, read the instructions carefully as it is easy to get confused between a header and footer and place your entries in the wrong box.

### 5.7.2  Creating Headers and Footers

1. *Click the View menu.*

2. *Click Header and Footer.*

3. *Click in the box that will appear and type your entry. This sets the header.*

4. *Click the mouse or Tab key to move across the box.*

5. *Click Switch Between Header and Footer to enter data in the Footer box.*

6. *Click the Close button to return to the document.*

Or

7. *Double click the grey document text that will be visible.*

8. *Double click a header or footer entry to return to this view.*

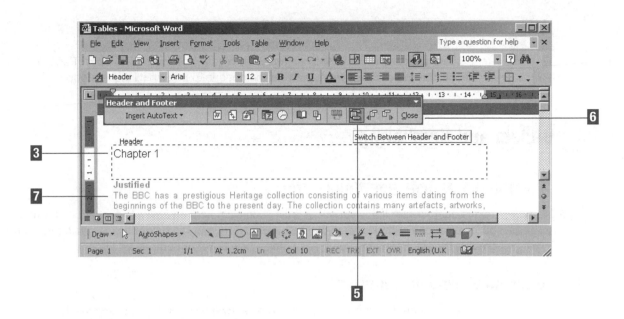

## 5.7.3 Inserting Automatic Fields

Use the following Header and Footer toolbar options to add entries into the header or footer boxes that will be updated automatically:

**1** *Page number*.

**2** *Date*.

**3** *Time*.

**4** *Click Insert AutoText for Filename, Author details etc.*

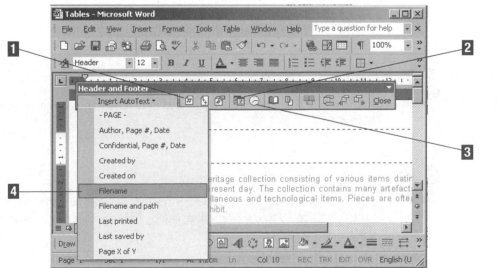

**The date looks wrong**

If the date appears as a US version (month before day) go to Start – Control Panel – Regional and Language Options and set the options to English (United Kingdom).

## 5.8 Bullets and Numbering

### 5.8.1 When to Use Bullets and Numbering

Text is often clearer if it is set out as a list, with each item on a new line introduced with a bullet point or a number. Items can be bulleted or numbered before typing or after you have created the list. Each time you press Enter, a new bullet or number will appear.

### 5.8.2 Applying Bullets or Numbers

1. *Select a ready-typed list or click on the page where you will start typing the list.*

2. *Click the Bullets toolbar button.*

Or

3. *Click the Numbering toolbar button.*

Or

4. *Click the Format menu.*

5. *Click Bullets and Numbering.*

6. *Click a style of bullet or number showing in the window.*

7. *Click None to take off bullets or numbers.*

8. *Click OK.*

**How do I continue typing without bullets?**

At the end of a list, press Enter to move onto a new line and then click off the toolbar button.

**Can I include non-bulleted items in a list?**

For a non-bulleted or numbered item in a list, click the line and click off the toolbar button. You could also move to that line by holding Shift as you press Enter.

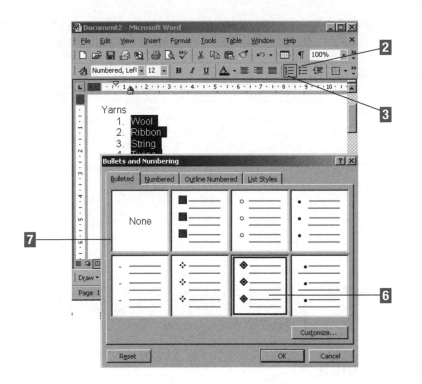

## 5.9 Indenting

### 5.9.1 Setting an Indent

**Assessment Objective 3i**

Text normally lines up on the left margin as you type. To move the text in from the margin, you must set an indent.

1. *Click the line or paragraph you want to indent.*

2. *Click the Increase Indent toolbar button. This moves the text to the right by 1.27 cm.*

3. *Keep clicking to move the text in further.*

4. *If you go too far, click the Decrease Indent toolbar button to reverse the indent.*

Or

5. *Click the Format menu.*

6. *Click Paragraph.*

7. *Use the arrows in the Left or Right indentation boxes or type your own measure to increase or decrease the indent.*

**5**

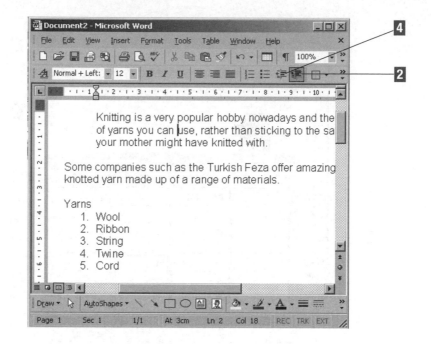

## 5.10 Word Count

### 5.10.1 Carrying Out a Word Count

Word can save a great deal of time by counting the number of pages, words, characters with or without spacing, paragraphs or lines in your document or any selected block of text.

To count the number of words:

1. *Select a block of text if you want to limit the count. Otherwise the count applies to the whole document.*

2. *Click the Tools menu.*

3. *Click Word Count.*

4. *Note the details displayed.*

# Formatting

## What You'll Do

→ Set font type

→ Set font size

→ Emphasise text

→ Insert paragraph breaks

→ Insert text

→ Move text

→ Delete text

→ Set line spacing

→ Replace text

## 6.1 Text Formatting

When you create a document, the appearance of the text will be set automatically in the software. To change the look of the text, or emphasise particular parts, you must change the default settings. This is known as formatting.

### 6.1.1 Selecting the Text

Once you have typed any text, you can change its appearance only by selecting it first. This tells the computer exactly which part of the document you want to change.

Selected text appears as white letters on a black background.

The weather report- selected text.

The weather report- unselected text.

There are a number of ways to select text in a document:

■ Double click to select a single word.

■ Triple click to select a paragraph.

■ Click at the start or end of a section and hold down the mouse button as you drag in the appropriate direction.

**6**

- Click the mouse in the left margin when the pointer displays a right facing arrow.

- With the arrow showing, hold down the button and drag the mouse to select several lines.

- Click in place and hold down the mouse button as you click an arrow (cursor) key to select characters or words to the left, right, above or below the cursor.

- Hold **Shift** and click an arrow key to select one character at a time.

- Click at the start of a long section, scroll down the page with the scroll bar and then hold **Shift** as you click at the end of the section. The entire section will be selected.

- Hold **Ctrl** and press **A**, or click the Edit menu and click Select All to select the entire document.

To take off a selection, click the mouse in the main area of the screen.

### How can I stop selecting too much text?

As you will be asked to format a specified block of text, take care not to 'overshoot' and select too many characters when using the mouse. If you find this has happened, keep the mouse button held down and drag the pointer slowly back up the words until only the required selection has been made.

## 6.1.2 Font Types

Assessment
Objective 4a

The appearance of text and numbers in word processed documents depends on the particular style of typeface that has been chosen. This is known as the font. Some examples of different fonts include:

- Arial
- Times New Roman
- Comic Sans MS
- ALGERIAN

To find out what font has been applied to any text:

1 *Click the text.*

2 *Check the name in the Font box on the formatting toolbar.*

3 *Its size will show in the Font Size box.*

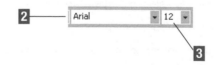

## 6.1.3  Setting Font Type

1. *Select the text to be changed, or click on screen.*

2. *Click the drop down arrow in the Font box.*

3. *Select an alternative font.*

Or

4. *Click the Format menu.*

5. *Click Font.*

6. *Select an alternative in the Font box.*

7. *Check the Preview.*

8. *Click OK.*

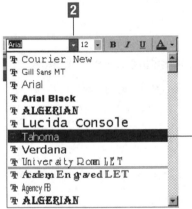

## 6.1.4  Setting Font Size

**Assessment Objective 4b**

1. *Select the text to be changed.*

2. *Click the drop down arrow in the Font Size box.*

3. *Select an alternative measure.*

4. *If the size is not offered, type your measure over that showing in the box.*

5. *Press Enter to confirm the size.*

Or

6. *Click the Format menu.*

7. *Click Font.*

8. *Select a measure in the Size box.*

9. *Click OK.*

---

### What font sizes should I use if the actual measure is not specified?

When asked to apply different font sizes, make sure they differ by at least two sizes and are large enough to read clearly.

---

## 6.1.5  Applying Emphasis

**Assessment Objective 4c**

To make any part of a document stand out, you can apply an emphasis to the font. You may want to:

- **Make it bold**

- *Make it italic*

- <u>Make it underlined</u>

Text without emphasis is known as Regular.

To apply emphasis:

1. *Select the text.*

2. *Click the B toolbar button for bold.*

3. *Click the I toolbar button for italic.*

4. *Click the U toolbar button for underlined.*

5. *Turn off the emphasis by clicking the button again.*

Or

6. *Click the Format menu.*

7. *Click Font.*

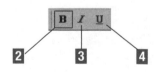

8. *Click an option in the Font style box.*

9. *Click OK.*

You can also use keyboard shortcuts for emphasis: **Ctrl–B** for bold, **Ctrl–I** for italic and **Ctrl–U** for underline.

## 6.2 Paragraph Breaks

### 6.2.1 Creating Paragraphs

**Assessment Objective 4d**

To create a paragraph, you need to move the text insertion point down two lines, so that you leave a clear line space before typing the second paragraph. You can do this at the end of any typing or within a block of text if you want to break it into two or more paragraphs.

1. *Click at the end of the last word you want in the first paragraph.*

2. *Press Enter once, to move the cursor onto the next line. Any text to the right of the cursor will move at the same time.*

3. *Press Enter again to insert a clear line space.*

4. *Start typing the new paragraph.*

### 6.2.2 Joining Paragraphs

If you don't want to retain separate paragraphs, join them up again by 'deleting' the space.

1. *Click at the beginning of the second paragraph.*

2. *Press the Backspace.*

Or

3. *Click at the end of the first paragraph.*

4. *Press the Delete key.*

## 6.3 Text Amendments

### 6.3.1 Inserting Text

1. *Click in the line where you want to add letters or words.*

**Assessment Objective 4e**

2. *Start typing. Extra characters will appear, pushing the existing text to the right.*

**6**

## Take care when inserting

It is easy to insert text in the wrong position.

## 6.3.2  Overtyping

If you find that existing type is being replaced when you try to insert new text, you have moved into Overtype mode. This happens when you press the Insert key by mistake.

☐1☐ Click Undo to add any characters that have been lost.

☐2☐ Press the Insert key on the keyboard to return to normal typing.

Or

☐3☐ Double click the symbol OVR that will have appeared in the status bar.

## 6.4  Moving or Copying Text

Assessment
Objective 4f

Earlier you learned how to move or copy files. Similar techniques are used to move or copy text to another part of the page, to other pages or to separate documents.

## Don't get confused!

A common mistake is to move instead of copy, or vice versa, or to move or copy text to the wrong position in the document. Make sure you move the accompanying punctuation as well as the text.

## 6.4.1  Moving or Copying Text by Dragging

☐1☐ *Select the text.*

☐2☐ *Move the pointer over the text until you see a white, right facing arrow.*

☐3☐ *To copy, hold down Ctrl. This will add a small box with a + sign in it.*

☐4☐ *Hold down the mouse button and drag the text to its new position. The arrow will display a small box.*

☐5☐ *The position of the text is shown by a dotted vertical bar.*

**The long, dusty and winding road**

6  *When the bar is in the correct position, let go of the mouse and the text (or a copy) will drop into place.*

7  *If necessary, adjust spacing between words.*

## 6.4.2  Moving or Copying Text Using Cut/Copy and Paste

1  *Select the text.*

2  *Click Cut to move it.*

Or

3  *Click Copy to copy it:*

   A  *Click the option on the Edit menu.*

   B  *Click the option after right clicking the text.*

Or

   C  *Click the toolbar button.*

4  *Click in the new position for the text.*

5  *Click Paste.*

You can also use the keyboard shortcuts **Ctrl–X** for Cut, **Ctrl–C** for Copy and **Ctrl–V** for Paste.

### Where do the words go when I cut them?

Text is copied temporarily into part of the computer memory known as the Clipboard. It can contain up to 24 items and you can paste anything from the Clipboard into a document over and over again. The Clipboard is emptied when you shut down the computer.

### Critical Error
**Failing to show evidence that you have moved the specified text or moving the wrong text.**

6

## 6.5 Deleting

### 6.5.1 Deleting Text

Unwanted text and associated punctuation can be deleted very easily.

1. *Select a block of text and press the Delete key.*

Or

2. *Click in place and then press the Backspace key to delete characters, spaces and punctuation to the left.*

3. *Press the Delete key to delete to the right.*

4. *Make sure any spacing is correct after a deletion.*

> ✕ **Critical Error**
> Failing to delete the specified text or deleting the wrong text.

## 6.6 Line Spacing

### 6.6.1 What is Line Spacing?

Normally as you type, new text will appear on the line below. This is single line spacing. To increase the gaps between lines, set different line spacing.

### 6.6.2 Changing Line Spacing

1. *Select the block of text to change.*

2. *Click an option from the line spacing toolbar button.*

3. *For extra options, click More . . .*

Or

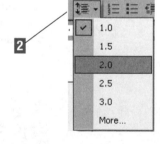

4. *Click the Format menu.*

5. *Click Paragraph.*

6. *Click an option in the Line spacing: box.*

7. *For an exact measure, type units into the At: box.*

8. *Click OK.*

A quick way to change line spacing is to hold **Ctrl** and press **2** for double line spacing, **5** for 1.5 spacing and **1** for single line spacing.

**Paragraph** dialog box

## The spacing doesn't look right

It may look odd to go from single to double line spacing, but don't worry if you have followed instructions correctly.

## 6.7 Finding and Replacing Text

### 6.7.1 The Role of Find and Replace

Assessment Objective 4i

Finding an entry in a long document can take time. Replacing text manually can also take time. Instead, you can use the find and replace tool available in Word. Replace is especially useful if you want to use an abbreviation for a long or complex word that can then be replaced automatically throughout the document before it is printed, or for correcting a mistake that has been made many times.

### 6.7.2 Using Find

1 *Click the Edit menu.*

2 *Click Find.*

3 *Type the entry in the Find what: box exactly as it appears in your document.*

4  *Click Find Next to display the first occurrence of the entry.*

5  *Keep clicking Find Next if there is a repeated entry you want to locate.*

6  *Click More (alternates with Less) to set criteria such as finding whole words only, matching case or searching in a specific direction.*

## 6.7.3 Using Replace

1  *Click the Edit menu.*

2  *Click Replace.*

Or

3  *Click the Replace tab in the Find and Replace box.*

4  *Type the word you are looking for in the Find what: box.*

5  *Type the replacement you want to make in the Replace with: box.*

6  *Click More to set specific criteria.*

7  *Click Replace All if you are sure all criteria are correct.*

8  *Click Find Next to check the first occurrence by eye.*

9  *Click Replace if it is correct.*

10  *Click Find Next to leave the word in place and continue searching.*

## What can go wrong?

Take care not to click Replace All when you have not first clicked 'Find whole words only'; parts of words may be replaced by mistake. Other common mistakes include replacing with an inaccurate word or failing to correct the spacing on either side of a word after a replacement.

## Learning outcomes

At the end of this unit, you should be able to:

→ Identify and use spreadsheet and graph software correctly

→ Use an input device to enter and edit data accurately

→ Insert, replicate and format arithmetical formulae

→ Use common numerical formatting and alignment

→ Manage and print spreadsheet documents and graph and chart documents

→ Produce pie charts, line graphs and bar/column charts

→ Select and present single and comparative sets of data

→ Set numerical parameters and format data

# CHAPTER 1

# Spreadsheet Basics

## What You'll Do

- ➡ Discover spreadsheets
- ➡ Launch Excel
- ➡ Close the application
- ➡ Start a new spreadsheet
- ➡ Open an existing spreadsheet
- ➡ Input text and numerical data
- ➡ Insert columns and rows
- ➡ Delete columns and rows
- ➡ Amend data

## 1.1 Discovering Spreadsheets

### 1.1.1 What are Spreadsheets?

A program such as Microsoft Excel will enable you to perform calculations on any figures that you enter. This means that you can use the program to keep track of financial or numerical information ranging from your bank account to shopping bills, scientific results, interest payments or your weight loss over time.

The main working area is a table of data known as a spreadsheet, but you can also display the contents of a spreadsheet in the form of a chart or graph.

### 1.1.2 Excel Files

An Excel file is referred to as a workbook and each 'page' is known as a worksheet. The term 'spreadsheet' is used for any worksheet where data has been set out in an understandable form. It is also often used as an alternative name for Excel files.

## 1.2 Working with Excel

### 1.2.1 Launching Excel

1. *Click the Start button*.

2. *Click All Programs*.

3. *Click Microsoft Excel*.

Or

4 *Click an icon or shortcut to the program if one is visible on the desktop.*

## 1.2.2 Closing Excel

1 *Click the Close button in the top, right hand corner of the window.*

Or

2 *Click the File menu.*

3 *Click Exit.*

## 1.2.3 Starting a New Spreadsheet

1 *Click the New button.*

Or

2 *Click the File menu.*

3 *Click New.*

4 *Click Blank Workbook in the New Workbook pane.*

New Workbook pane

## 1.2.4 Opening an Existing Spreadsheet

<kbd>1</kbd> *Click the Open toolbar button* .

Or

<kbd>2</kbd> *Click the File menu.*

<kbd>3</kbd> *Click Open.*

<kbd>4</kbd> *Navigate to the appropriate folder.*

<kbd>5</kbd> *Click the file name.*

<kbd>6</kbd> *Click Open or press Enter.*

Or

<kbd>7</kbd> *If the New Workbook pane is open, click the name of a recent workbook.*

---

**ⓘ Are there any quicker methods to open files?**

A list of recently opened spreadsheets will be available at the bottom of the File menu.

---

## 1.3 Creating a Spreadsheet

## 1.3.1 The Excel Screen

When Excel opens, you will see a grid of columns and rows as well as toolbars and menus.

<kbd>1</kbd> Each column is labelled with a letter of the alphabet.

<kbd>2</kbd> Each row is numbered.

<kbd>3</kbd> Each square is known as a cell.

<kbd>4</kbd> The cell with a black border is the *active* cell and any typing will appear inside it.

<kbd>5</kbd> The bar across the top of the cells is the Formula bar. The contents of the active cell will appear here.

<kbd>6</kbd> Each cell is referred to by its column letter and row number. The cell reference of the active cell appears in the Name Box.

<kbd>7</kbd> There are tabs at the bottom of the screen to move between sheets.

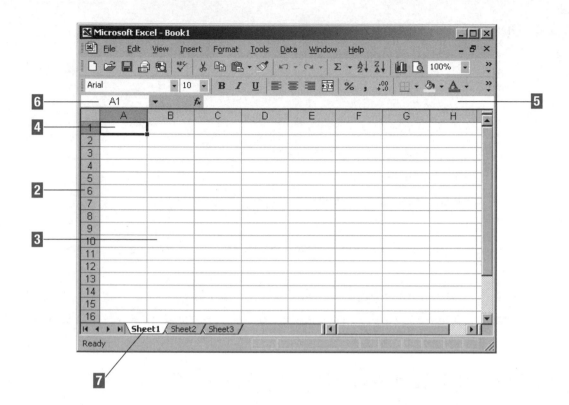

## 1.3.2 The Active Cell

When you open Excel, the active cell is always A1. To enter text or numbers into a different cell, you must activate it.

1. *Click the mouse in any cell.*

2. *Press the Tab key to move across the row to the right.*

3. *Press Enter to move down a row.*

4. *Press Home to move to column A in the current row.*

5. *Press **Ctrl–Home** to return to cell A1.*

6. *Press an arrow (cursor) key to move in any direction.*

## 1.3.3 Entering Text and Numbers

Assessment
Objective 1a

1. *Click the active cell and start typing.*

2. *Entries will appear inside the cell and also in the Formula bar.*

3. *Confirm the entry by activating another cell.*

Or

4. *Click the green tick in the Formula bar.*

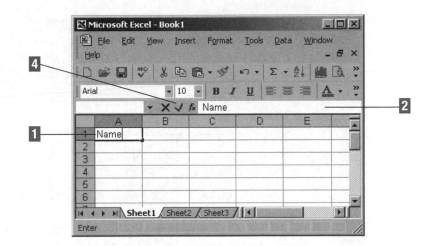

> **Critical Error**
> Entering numerical data incorrectly.

## 1.4 Inserting Columns and Rows

**Assessment
Objective 1b**

After creating a spreadsheet that has a number of columns and rows, it is common to find that extra data needs to be added. This means you must add one or more new columns or rows.

Many people confuse columns with rows. Columns have heading *letters* and go vertically up and down the worksheet, rows have heading *numbers* and go horizontally across the worksheet.

### 1.4.1 Inserting a Column

 Click the heading letter to the right of the position for the new column.

2 Click and drag across a number of heading letters if you want to insert that number of columns.

3 Click the Insert menu.

4 Click Columns.

5 A new column will slide into place and heading letters will be adjusted automatically.

![Microsoft Excel screenshot showing the Insert menu open with Columns highlighted, and a spreadsheet containing Title, First name, Surname, Town, Age columns]

Microsoft Excel - Book1

File   Edit   View   Insert   Format   Tools   Data   Window

Help

Rows
Columns ———————————— 4
Worksheet
Name ▶

Arial

D1

| | A | B | C | D | E |
|---|---|---|---|---|---|
| 1 | Title | First name | Surname | Town | Age |
| 2 | Mr | Peter | Brown | Sheffield | 46 |
| 3 | Mrs | Mary | Green | Birmingham | 33 |
| 4 | Ms | Sheila | Lacy | Manchester | 56 |
| 5 | Mr | Steven | Collins | Bradford | 43 |
| 6 | | | | | |
| 7 | | | | | |
| 8 | | | | | |
| 9 | | | | | |
| 10 | | | | | |

Sheet1  Sheet2  Sheet3

Ready

5

| | C | D | E |
|---|---|---|---|
| | Surname | Postc | Town |
| | Brown | | Sheffield |
| | Green | | Birmingham |
| | Lacy | | Manchester |
| | Collins | | Bradford |

## 1.4.2  Inserting a Row

1. Click the heading number of the row below the position for the new row.

2. Click and drag across a number of heading numbers to insert that number of new rows.

3. Click the Insert menu.

4. Click Rows.

A quick way to insert a column or row is to select the column to the right or the row below, hold **Ctrl** and press the + key.

 **Critical Error**
Not inserting the correct column or row.

**The column appeared in the wrong place!**

Take care that you insert the column or row in the correct position. If it does not have the correct letter or number, delete it and start again.

## 1.5 Deleting Columns and Rows

Selecting the contents of a column or row and pressing Delete will remove only cell contents, not the entire column or row. This means heading letters and numbers will not be adjusted.

### 1.5.1 Deleting a Column

1. *Click the heading letter to select the entire column.*

2. *Click the Edit menu.*

3. *Click Delete.*

### 1.5.2 Deleting a Row

1. *Click the row heading number.*

2. *Click the Edit menu.*

3. *Click Delete.*

A quick way to delete a column or row is to select it, hold **Ctrl** and press the subtract or minus key.

**Critical Error**
Deleting the wrong column or row, or not deleting the specified column or row.

## 1.6 Making Amendments

If you notice a mistake, or want to change an entry, you must either break into the cell or use the Formula bar to make your amendments.

### 1.6.1 Amending Data

1. *If you have just typed something wrongly, click the red cross in the Formula bar to cancel the typing.*

2. *Click any cell you want to edit.*

3 *Press Delete to remove the entire contents.*

4 *Click in the Formula bar to edit an entry.*

Or

5 *Double click the cell to place the cursor inside for editing.*

6 *Use the Delete and Backspace keys and enter new data as normal.*

7 *Click another cell or the green tick in the Formula bar to accept the changes.*

### Check and check again

Remember that inaccurate numerical data, whether entered originally or after an amendment, is penalised as a critical error. You should also take care to check your text for spelling mistakes as you are allowed only four data entry errors in a New CLAIT assessment.

CHAPTER 2

# Using Formulae

## What You'll Do

→ Understand the structure of a formula

→ Discover functions

→ Select a cell range

→ Replicate formulae

→ Recalculate data

**2**

## 2.1 The Structure of a Formula

Calculations are performed when you type the correct formula into a cell and then press Enter or activate another cell. Results are displayed in the cell and the underlying formula is displayed in the Formula bar.

You can add, subtract, multiply or divide any numbers, as well as numerical data that has been entered into a spreadsheet. As the data will be in discrete cells, you can either:

**1** Use the exact figures.

**2** Replace these with the cell references.

(Microsoft Excel - Book1 window)

| | A | B | C | D |
|---|---|---|---|---|
| 1 | 245 | 76 | =245+76 | |
| 2 | 245 | 76 | =A2+B2 | |
| 3 | | | | |
| 4 | | | | |
| 5 | | | | |

**1**

**2**

If you use actual figures, you will have to redo the calculation if the figures change. If you use cell references, the calculation will be updated automatically. This is because Excel uses the contents of a cell *at that time* in any calculation.

## 2.1.1 Performing a Calculation

Assessment
Objective 2a

1. *Click in the cell where the result will be displayed.*

2. *Press =.*

3. *Enter a number.*

Or

4. *Enter the cell reference for the first number.*

5. *Enter the operator.*

6. *Enter a number.*

Or

7. *Enter the cell reference for the second number.*

8. *Repeat with more entries if necessary and then press Enter, click another cell or click the tick in the Formula bar.*

9. *Check the formula in the Formula bar if the result appears wrong.*

Excel recognises the following four operators:

+ for addition (e.g. = A1+B1)

- for subtraction (e.g. = A1-B1)

* for multiplication (e.g. = A1*B1)

/ for divide (e.g. = A1/B1)

### 2.1.2 Adding a Cell Reference to a Formula

1. *Type it in manually.*

Or

2. *Click the cell with the mouse. Flashing lines will appear round the cell and its cell reference will be added to the formula automatically.*

**I have clicked too many times!**

Take care when creating formulae using the mouse. If you click extra cells, their cell references will be added. If this happens, cancel the formula and start again.

**Do you have to use capital letters?**

When typing cell references, you can use either lower case or capital letters – Excel will change them to capitals.

## 2.1.3 BODMAS

Excel follows normal mathematical conventions when it performs calculations, with operations carried out in a specific order no matter where they appear in a formula.

1st – figures in **b**rackets, e.g. 2/3 – **(10*5.5)**

2nd – **o**rder (raised to the power), e.g. $3 * 2^4 + 25$

3rd – **d**ivision and **m**ultiplication, working from left to right, e.g. **1*7** – 3 – **4/2**

4th – **a**ddition and **s**ubtraction, working from left to right.

Knowing this means:

1. You will understand the result you are going to get.

2. If you have a formula where an operation such as addition must be carried out first, it should be enclosed in brackets.

## 2.2 Functions

Some calculations are performed so regularly that Excel offers a range of pre-defined formulae known as functions that will carry them out automatically. These include:

SUM – total a range of cells.

AVERAGE – average a range of cells.

MAX – identify the highest figure in a range.

MIN – identify the lowest figure in a range.

COUNT – count up how many cells in the range contain numbers.

You can click the AutoSum toolbar button $\Sigma$ ▾ to enter the SUM function automatically, and other functions are available from a drop down list next to it.

## 2.2.1 Selecting a Cell Range

To perform calculations on a number of cells, you must select them first.

**1** *Click the first cell when the pointer shows a white cross.*

**2** *Hold down the mouse button and drag the pointer down a column or across a row.*

**3** *Let go and they will all be selected: cell contents will be shaded blue and have a black border.*

**4** *The first cell will remain white, rather than shaded, but it will be included in the selection.*

## 2.2.2 Using the SUM Function

**1** *Select the range of cells you want to total.*

**2** *Click the AutoSum button on the toolbar.*

**3** *The total will appear in the next empty cell.*

Or

**4** *Enter the function from the keyboard, remembering to include the colon between the cell references:*

**=SUM(first cell reference in range: last cell reference in range)**

You could also enter **=SUM**(and then drag across the cell range with the mouse to add the cell references between the brackets).

**5** *Press Enter and the total will appear.*

**Should I always use SUM for totals?**

When totalling just a few cells you can choose between SUM and normal addition if no method is specified. A formula such as =A3+A4+A5 does *not* require brackets. For a larger range, always use the SUM function.

## 2.2.3 Using the AVERAGE Function

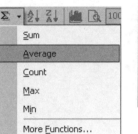

[1] Select the cell range.

[2] Click the drop down arrow next to the AutoSum button and select Average.

Or

[3] Click in the cell where you want the result to appear.

[4] Type =AVERAGE( .

[5] Drag the mouse across the range of cells to add their cell references to the formula.

[6] Press Enter.

| | A | B | C | D | E | F |
|---|---|---|---|---|---|---|
| 1 | Item | Number sold | Cost per item | Total price | | |
| 2 | Writing pad | 22 | £6.50 | £143.00 | | |
| 3 | Notebook | 14 | £3.00 | £42.00 | | |
| 4 | Sketch pad | 17 | £7.45 | £126.65 | | |
| 5 | Box of pencils | 3 | £9.50 | £28.50 | | |
| 6 | Box of crayons | 7 | £11.50 | £80.50 | | |
| 7 | TOTAL | | | £420.65 | | |
| 8 | AVERAGE PRICE | | =AVERAGE(C2:C6 | | | |

Microsoft Excel - Book2
File  Edit  View  Insert  Format  Tools  Data  Window  Help
STEYX    fx =AVERAGE(C2:C6
Sheet1 / Sheet2 / Sheet3
Point

**Critical Error**
Using incorrect formulae that produce the wrong result or displaying the results in the wrong position.

Note that you will be penalised if you use a formula instead of a function where this is specified.

## 2.3 Replicating Formulae

Assessment
Objective 2b

If you are carrying out the same calculation in a number of rows or columns, you can copy the formula from one cell to the next. This makes use of *relative* cell references as the formula will adjust as you move from one column or row to the next.

In the example, copying the formula in A3 to B3 will mean that the formula will now refer to cells in column B. Copy again and the formula will refer to cells in column C.

|   | A | B | C |
|---|---|---|---|
| 1 | 200 | 300 | 250 |
| 2 | 26 | 22 | 15 |
| 3 | =A1*A2 | =B1*B2 | =C1*C2 |

### 2.3.1 Replicating Formulae Using AutoFill

1 *Enter the first formula in the normal way.*

2 *Click the cell containing the formula.*

3 *Move the pointer over a small black square visible in the bottom, right hand corner of the cell – the fill handle.*

4 *When the pointer changes to a black cross, click and drag the cross down the column or across the row.*

5 *Dotted lines will show where the formulae are being copied.*

6 *Let go of the mouse and the cells will fill with the new calculations.*

|   | A | B | C | D |
|---|---|---|---|---|
| 1 | Item | Number sold | Cost per item | Total Cost |
| 2 | Writing pad | 22 | £6.50 | £143.00 |
| 3 | Notebook | 14 | £3.00 | |
| 4 | Sketch pad | 17 | £7.45 | |
| 5 | Box of pencils | 3 | £9.50 | |
| 6 | Box of crayons | 7 | £11.50 | |
| 7 | TOTAL | | | |

### 2.3.2 Replicating Formulae Using the Menu

1 *Enter the first formula.*

2 *Select the range of cells for the calculation, including the cell containing the original formula.*

3  Click the Edit menu.

4  Click Fill.

5  Click Down for columns and Right for rows.

6  You can also replicate formulae up or left.

**Warning**

All replicated (copied) formulae must match the structure of the source formula. Don't avoid replicating and enter formulae manually as you are likely to make mistakes.

## 2.4 Recalculating Data

**Assessment Objective 2c**

Every time numerical data on a spreadsheet is changed, calculations containing a reference to amended cells will be updated automatically.

### 2.4.1 Updating Formulae

- If you insert new columns or rows, calculations based on functions such as SUM will take into account new figures, as the formula refers to all cells between the first and the last in a range.

- If you have totalled cells using simple addition, the total will not be updated automatically and you will have to add new cell references to the formula manually.

**Critical Error**
Not updating formulae after columns and rows have been inserted.

# CHAPTER 3

# Producing Charts and Graphs

## What You'll Do

→ Distinguish between different types of chart and graph

→ Create charts and graphs

→ Select different data sets

## 3.1 What are Charts and Graphs?

These are graphical representations of spreadsheet data. You must have a spreadsheet on which to base the chart or graph and select all or part of the data before starting the chart creation process.

Charts can be placed on the same worksheet as the data or on their own worksheet. To make charts easier to locate, rename the sheets during or after chart creation, or the tabs will be labelled Chart1, Chart2 etc.

### 3.1.1 Renaming a Worksheet

**1** *Double click the sheet tab.*

**2** *Type your preferred name over the highlighted name.*

**3** *Press Enter to confirm the naming.*

**4** *Navigate to a different sheet by clicking the tab name.*

Or

**5** *Click a navigation arrow to reveal further sheets.*

## 3.2 Different Types of Chart and Graph

Excel offers a wide range of complex charts and graphs, but for New CLAIT you need only to be able to identify and create four simple types and should create 2D rather than 3D examples:

**2D column chart**

**2D bar chart**

**Pie chart**

**Line graph**

**Critical Error**
Selecting a stacked chart or graph.

### 3.2.1 Parts of a Chart

The various parts of a chart or graph that you need to recognise are:

**1** Chart title.

**2** Axis title.

**3** X-axis label.

**4** Y-axis value.

**5** Plot area.

**6** Chart area.

**7** Data series – represented by bars, pie chart slices or lines.

**8** Legend (key).

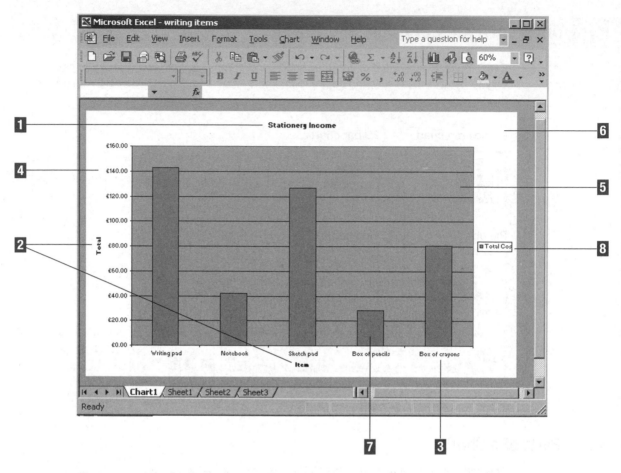

Note that in a bar chart, the vertical axis is the X-axis.

## 3.3 Creating Charts and Graphs

**Assessment Objective 3a**

There are two ways to create a graph or chart – by working through the wizard or by using a shortcut. Once in place, you will find you can customise fonts, colours, lines and other parts. How to do this is described in the next chapter.

### 3.3.1 Creating a Chart Using the Wizard

**1** *Open the data file containing the spreadsheet on which the chart or graph will be based.*

**2** *Select the correct data. Include column and row headings but not main titles or totals.*

**3** *Click the Chart Wizard button.*

**4** *Step 1: Click the style of chart you want to create.*

5 Click the Sample button to preview its appearance.

6 Click Next.

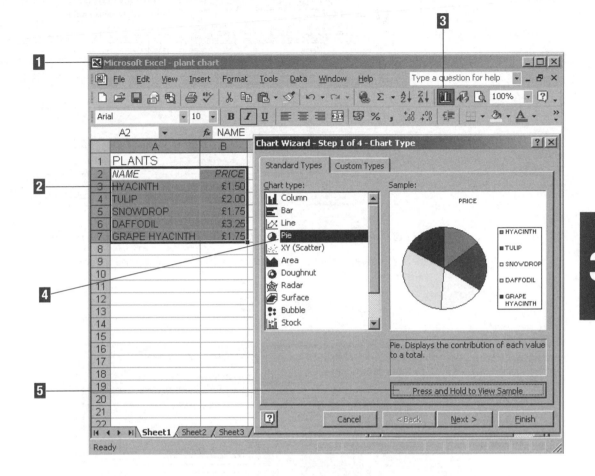

7 Step 2: Check that the source data is correct. If not, cancel the chart and re-select the data. When you are ready, click Next.

**Critical Error**
Displaying data on the incorrect axis.

8 Step 3: On the Titles tab, enter chart and axis titles. They will appear automatically on the chart.

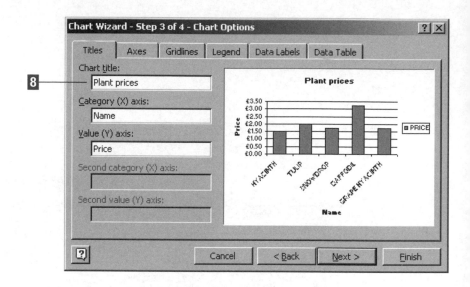

9  Click the Data Labels tab to add values, percentages or names to the chart or graph.

10  Click the Legend tab if you want to remove or re-position the legend.

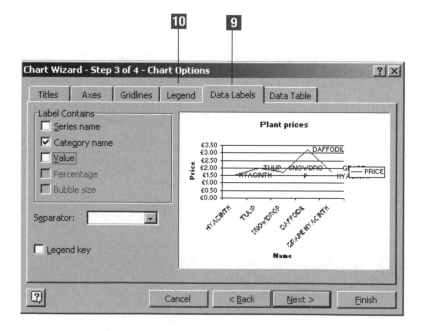

11  Step 4: Click the radio button for the sheet on which to place the chart. You can rename the sheet at this point if placing it on its own worksheet. Otherwise, it will be named Chart1.

12  Click Finish and the chart will appear.

**Chart Wizard - Step 4 of 4 - Chart Location**

Place chart:

As new sheet: `Plant char`

As object in: `Sheet1`

Cancel    < Back    Next >    Finish

## 3.3.2 Creating a Chart Using the Keyboard

1. *Select the data.*

2. *Press function key F11.*

3. *A column chart will appear on its own sheet.*

4. *If you want a different type of chart:*

    A. *Right click in the white chart area.*

    B. *Click Chart Types.*

    C. *Select a different type of chart.*

    D. *Click OK.*

### Where has my data gone?

The original data you used to create your chart will still be on the original sheet, normally Sheet1, so return there if necessary by clicking the sheet tab.

## 3.4 Displaying Data

Charts or graphs created on a separate sheet normally display well, but if you add one to the same worksheet holding the data, it may appear too small to see clearly.

## 3.4.1 Working with Selected Charts

1. *Click the chart or graph to select it. It will show a black border and small boxes (sizing handles) round the edge.*

2. *Resize the chart – click on a sizing handle and drag out the boundary with the mouse.*

3. *Move a chart – click on the centre and drag it to a new position on the sheet.*

## 3.4.2 Deleting Charts and Graphs

1. *Select a chart or graph that is on the same sheet as the data.*

2. *Press the Delete key.*

3. *If it is on its own worksheet, click the Edit menu.*

4. *Click Delete sheet.*

# 3.5 Selecting Different Data Sets

**Assessment Objective 3b**

You can select a wide range of different data sets on which to base charts or graphs. It is common to select a subset of the data, or to compare two different sets of similar data.

| | A | B | C | D | E | F | G |
|---|---|---|---|---|---|---|---|
| 1 | PLANTS | | | | | | |
| 2 | *NAME* | *NUMBER BOUGHT* | *PRICE* | *COST* | | | |
| 3 | HYACINTH | 3 | £1.50 | £4.50 | | | |
| 4 | TULIP | 10 | £2.00 | £20.00 | | | |
| 5 | SNOWDROP | 14 | £1.75 | £24.50 | | | |
| 6 | DAFFODIL | 8 | £3.25 | £26.00 | | | |
| 7 | GRAPE HYACINTH | 16 | £1.75 | £28.00 | | | |
| 8 | | | | | | | |
| 9 | | | | | Compare the price of two plants | | |
| 10 | Compare the numbers of two plants bought | | | | *NAME* | *PRICE* | |
| 11 | *NAME* | *NUMBER BOUGHT* | | | HYACINTH | £1.50 | |
| 12 | HYACINTH | 3 | | | TULIP | £2.00 | |
| 13 | TULIP | 10 | | | | | |
| 14 | | | | | | | |
| 15 | | | | | Compare the cost of 4 plants | | |
| 16 | Compare the numbers of all the plants bought | | | | *NAME* | *COST* | |
| 17 | *NAME* | *NUMBER BOUGHT* | | | HYACINTH | £4.50 | |
| 18 | HYACINTH | 3 | | | TULIP | £20.00 | |
| 19 | TULIP | 10 | | | SNOWDROP | £24.50 | |
| 20 | SNOWDROP | 14 | | | DAFFODIL | £26.00 | |
| 21 | DAFFODIL | 8 | | | | | |
| 22 | GRAPE HYACINTH | 16 | | | | | |

**Critical Error**

Selecting an incorrect row or column of data, or producing a chart or graph with missing data or values.

## 3.5.1 Selecting Non-adjacent Cell Ranges

1. *Select the first range with the mouse.*

2. *Hold **Ctrl** and select subsequent ranges. All will remain selected.*

| | A | B | C | D |
|---|---|---|---|---|
| 1 | PLANTS | | | |
| 2 | *NAME* | *NUMBER BOUGHT* | *PRICE* | *COST* |
| 3 | HYACINTH | 3 | £1.50 | £4.50 |
| 4 | TULIP | 10 | £2.00 | £20.00 |
| 5 | SNOWDROP | 14 | £1.75 | £24.50 |
| 6 | DAFFODIL | 8 | £3.25 | £26.00 |
| 7 | GRAPE HYACINTH | 16 | £1.75 | £28.00 |

# CHAPTER 4

# Formatting

## What You'll Do

→ Align text and numerical data

→ Format numerical data

→ Widen columns

→ Add borders and shading

→ Set and amend chart and graph titles

→ Display data labels

→ Use a legend

→ Ensure comparative data is distinct

## 4.1 What Can You Format?

Spreadsheets can be confusing, so many people like to improve the appearance by emphasising headings, adding colours and borders and re-aligning entries.

More importantly, numerical data can be displayed in different ways without changing its underlying value by applying number formats. These include currency, percentages, a different number of decimal places or the style of date or time.

Charts and graphs can also be formatted so that comparative data is easier to read and labels and titles are clearer.

## 4.2 Aligning Text and Numerical Data

**Assessment Objective 4a**

When you type into a cell, text will always appear on the left and numerical data will appear on the right. To change this display, you must re-align the entries.

### 4.2.1 Changing Alignment

1. Click the cell, or select a range of cells.

2. Click the appropriate alignment button on the toolbar – a) left, b) centre or c) right align.

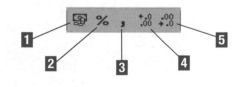

# 4.3 Formatting Numerical Data

Assessment
Objective 4b
You can use the normal formatting buttons to select a different font and font size and apply bold or italic emphasis or underline any text or numerical entries. There are toolbar buttons for formatting numerical data or you can use the options on the Format menu.

## 4.3.1 Numerical Formats on the Toolbar

Click a cell or select a range of cells and click the appropriate toolbar button for many of the formats:

1 Currency.

2 Percentage.

3 1000s separator.

4 Increase decimal places.

5 Decrease decimal places.

### Applying a percentage format

Take care with percentages. These are applied to decimals. A whole number such as 24 in a cell formatted to percentage will appear as 2400%.

## 4.3.2 Formatting Numbers Using the Menu

1. *Right click and select Format Cells.*

Or

2. *Click the Format menu.*

3. *Click Cells.*

4. *On the Number tab, click the Number category.*

5. *For numbers, currency or percentage, click in the Decimal places box to set the numbers displayed.*

6. *Set 0 decimal places for an integer (whole number).*

7. *Check the sample.*

8. *Click the separator box if you want thousands separated.*

9. *For currency, click the Symbol box to take off a £ symbol or select a different currency symbol.*

10. *For Date and Time set a long (1st May 2007) or short (1/5/07) date.*

11. *Click OK to apply the formatting.*

## 4.4 Resizing Columns and Rows

Assessment
Objective 4c

After typing a long entry into one cell, some of it will disappear from view if there are any entries in the next column. You need to widen the column to display the contents in full. You may also want a deeper row height.

Select a number of columns or rows to resize them at the same time.

### 4.4.1 Resizing Columns and Rows Using the Mouse

1. *Move the pointer to the grey column heading letter or row heading number.*

2. *Position it over the right hand boundary of the column.*

Or

3. *On the lower row boundary.*

4. *Click and hold down the mouse button when the pointer shows a two-way arrow.*

**Row height**

5. *Drag the column boundary to the right.*

Or

6. *Drag the row boundary down.*

7. *The actual measure will be displayed.*

**4**

### 4.4.2  Using AutoFit

You can size a column or row to fit the widest or highest entry exactly.

1. *Position the pointer over the right hand column boundary to the right of the column letter.*

Or

2. *Over the row boundary below the row number.*

3. *Double click the mouse when the pointer shows a two-way arrow.*

### 4.4.3  Resizing Using the Menu

1. *Click a cell or select a column or row.*

2. *Click the Format menu.*

3. *Click Column or Row.*

4. *Click an option:*

   A. *Width or Height – type in an exact measure.*

   B. *Standard width – the default settings.*

   C. *AutoFit – sets it to the longest or highest entry.*

 **Critical Error**
Not displaying numerical data in full.

 **What does a row of ### mean?**
If you perform a calculation and see these symbols appear in the cell, it just means the column is too narrow to display the results. Widen the column to remove the symbols.

## 4.5  Borders and Shading

Assessment
Objective 4c
To make parts of a spreadsheet stand out, border the cells with a thick or coloured line or shade the cell background.

### 4.5.1  Applying Borders from the Toolbar

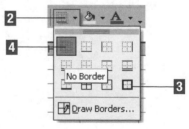

1. *Select the cells.*

2. *Click the drop down arrow next to the Borders toolbar button.*

3. *Click a style of border.*

4. *Remove an unwanted border by clicking the No Border option.*

## 4.5.2 Applying Borders Using the Menu

> 1. Select the cells.
>
> 2. Right click and select Format Cells.
>
> 3. Click Border.
>
> 4. Click a preset type of border such as Outline for an outer border or Inside for a grid.
>
> 5. Remove an unwanted border by clicking None.
>
> 6. Click a style of border line.
>
> 7. Click the drop down arrow in the colour box to colour the line.
>
> 8. Click OK.

## 4.5.3 Applying Shading

> 1. Select the cells.
>
> 2. Click the drop down arrow next to the Fill Color toolbar button to select a colour.

Or

> 3. Right click and select Format Cells.
>
> 4. Click Patterns.
>
> 5. Click a coloured square.
>
> 6. Remove colour by clicking No Color.
>
> 7. Click OK.

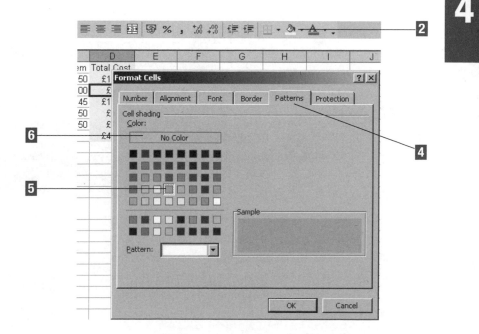

## 4.6 | Setting and Amending Chart and Graph Titles

**Assessment Objective 4d**

When using the Chart Wizard, you enter titles at Step 3. You can also amend titles or add new ones to a completed chart or graph.

### 4.6.1 Adding Titles

1. *Right click the white chart area.*

2. *Click Chart Options.*

3. *Complete the chart and axes title boxes.*

4. *Click OK.*

### 4.6.2 Amending Titles

1. *Click the title.*

2. *Drag the title if you want it in a different position on the chart.*

3. *Type into the box to edit the text.*

4. *Use normal formatting options to change font, font size or emphasis if the title is not clear.*

Or

5. *Right click the title and select the Format Chart Title option.*

6. *Change settings in the Font box.*

> ### Critical Error
> Failing to add a title or using one that does not identify the chart correctly.

## 4.7 Scale

**Assessment Objective 4e** When a chart or graph appears, Excel will set the Y-axis values and the intervals between them. If you want to change the values displayed, you must change the scale.

### 4.7.1 Setting Axes' Upper and Lower Limits

[1] *Right click the Y-axis.*

[2] *Click Format Axis.*

[3] *Click the Scale tab.*

[4] *Enter new figures into the Minimum (lowest value) and Maximum (highest value) boxes.*

[5] *If necessary, enter a new interval – the major unit.*

[6] *Click OK.*

---

**Critical Error**
Making a change to the upper or lower limits that results in missing data.

## 4.8 Displaying Data Labels

**Assessment Objective 4f**

Adding data labels to a pie chart will add category names, values or percentages to the pie slices. On a column chart or graph, it adds labels to points along the line or to the top of the columns.

### 4.8.1 Adding Data Labels

1. *Click the Data Labels tab at Step 3 of the Chart Wizard when creating a chart.*

Or

2. *Right click the white chart area.*

3. *Click Chart Options.*

4. *Click the Data Labels tab.*

5. *Click in the checkboxes for the labels you want to display.*

6. *Click OK.*

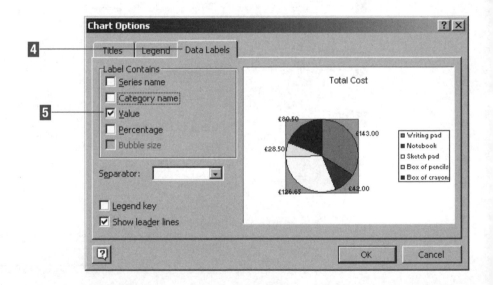

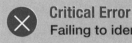
**Critical Error**
Failing to identify the data clearly with appropriate labels.

## 4.9 Using a Legend

Assessment
Objective 4g

When creating a graph or chart, the legend will appear automatically. You can remove or reinstate it if asked to do so.

### 4.9.1 Removing a Legend

1 *Click the legend.*

2 *Press Delete.*

### 4.9.2 Adding a Legend

1 *Right click the white chart area.*

2 *Click Chart Options.*

3 *Click the Legend tab.*

4 *Click to place a tick in the Show Legend box.*

5 *Click an alternative placement option.*

6 *Click OK.*

## 4.10 Ensuring Comparative Data is Distinct

Assessment
Objective 4h

There is no requirement to print charts or graphs in colour. This means some bars or lines may appear similar in greyscale. Make sure they are distinct by preparing for a greyscale printout and/or increasing contrast, widening or restyling lines or adding or changing line markers.

**4**

### Do I always need a legend?

When printing comparative data, ensure that a legend is visible on the chart or graph to help make the data distinct.

### 4.10.1 Making Comparative Data Distinctive

1 *Click a single data point such as a column, bar or pie chart slice.*

2 *Right click a line or selected data point.*

3 *Click Format Data.*

4 *On the Patterns tab, click in the Color box for a different line colour.*

5 *Click in the Weight box to select a different width.*

6 *Click in the Style box to select a dotted or block line.*

**7** For markers, click None to remove a marker.

**8** Click in the Style, Size and Foreground/Background boxes to make other changes.

**9** Click OK.

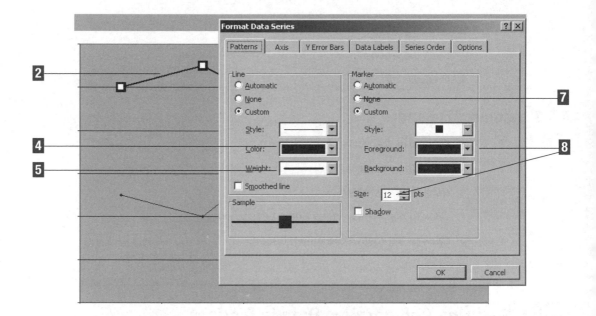

## 4.10.2 Printing Comparative Data in Black and White

**1** *Click the File menu.*

**2** *Click Page Setup.*

**3** *Click the Chart tab.*

**4** *Click to place a tick in the Print in black and white checkbox. This changes colours to patterns.*

**5** *Click OK.*

> **✕ Critical Error**
> Failing to identify comparative data clearly.

# CHAPTER 5

# Saving and Printing

## What You'll Do

→ Save and close a spreadsheet

→ Set page layout

→ Add headers and footers

→ Print a spreadsheet

→ Show underlying formulae

→ Display spreadsheet row and column headings

→ Print charts and graphs on a separate sheet

## 5.1 Saving and Closing a Spreadsheet

**Assessment Objective 5a**

Charts and graphs are part of an Excel workbook file so that if they are on their own sheet, this will be treated like any other worksheet and will be saved when the file is named and saved.

You must rename a file, or save it to a new location, if you want to retain the original while you work on a new version.

### 5.1.1 Saving a Spreadsheet

**1** *Click the Save button.*

Or

**2** *Click the File menu.*

**3** *Click Save.*

**4** *Select a suitable location for the file so that it shows in the Save in: box.*

**5** *Edit the file name, making sure you enter it accurately.*

**6** *Click Save or press Enter.*

You can use the shortcut **Ctrl–S** instead of clicking the Save button.

 Update your work regularly by clicking Save to save any changes you make to your workbooks.

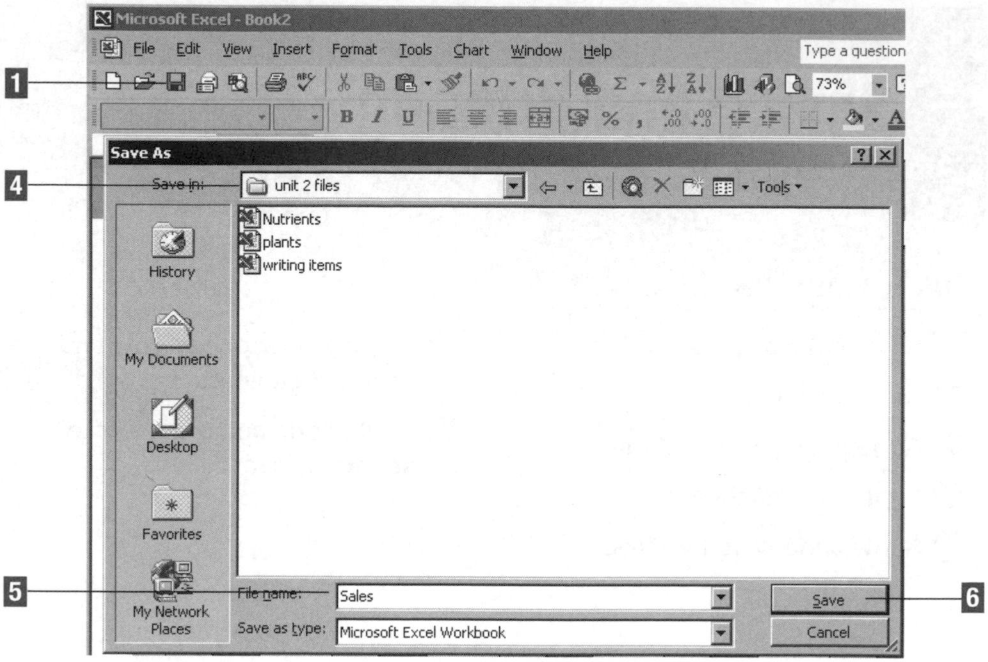


## 5.1.2 Saving a Different Version

1 *Click the File menu.*

2 *Click Save As.*

3 *Edit the file name and/or select a different location in the Save in: box.*

4 *Click Save.*

## 5.1.3 Closing a Spreadsheet

1 *Click the lower Close button in the window.*

Or

2 *Click the File menu.*

3 *Click Close.*

4 *If you click the upper Close button you will exit Excel.*

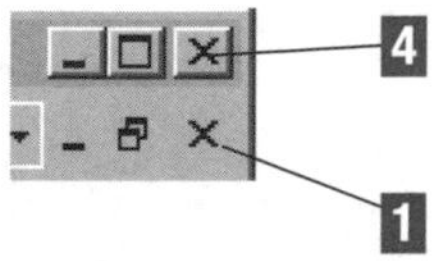

## 5.2 | Preparing to Print

Assessment
Objective 5b

If you press the Print button 🖨 you will print a single copy of the active spreadsheet or chart in portrait orientation using the default settings. These can all be changed to suit your particular needs.

### 5.2.1 Using Print Preview

To see what the spreadsheet or chart will look like before and after you change settings, view it in Print Preview.

[1] Click the Print Preview button 🔍.

Or

[2] Click the File menu.

[3] Click Print Preview.

[4] Leave the preview by clicking the Close button.

[5] You can go directly to the Print or Page Setup boxes from this view.

## 5.3 | Margins

You won't often want to position a spreadsheet exactly on the page, but if you do you can change the width of the margins round the edge of your data.

### 5.3.1 Changing Margins Using the Menu

[1] Click the File menu.

[2] Click Page Setup.

[3] Click the Margins tab.

[4] Change units in any of the boxes.

[5] Click to set the spreadsheet horizontally and/or vertically in the centre of the page.

[6] Click OK.

5

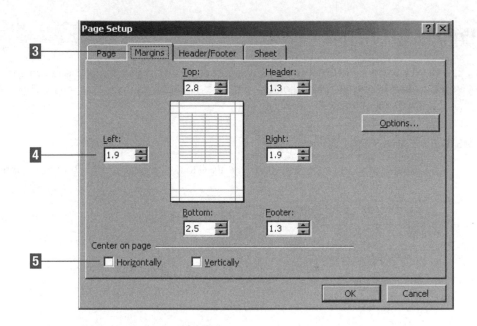

## 5.3.2  Changing Margins Using the Mouse

1  *Click the Print Preview button.*

2  *Click the Margins button.*

3  *Click and drag any of the margin lines that appear when the pointer shows a two-way arrow.*

4  *Click OK.*

## 5.4  Page Orientation

Spreadsheets often have so many columns that they will extend across a number of pages when printed out in portrait orientation. It is usually necessary to change to landscape orientation.

## 5.4.1  Changing Page Orientation

1  *Click the File menu.*

2  *Click Page Setup.*

3  *Click the Page tab.*

4  *Click in the Landscape Orientation radio button.*

5  *Click OK.*

## 5.5 | Gridlines

Depending on your computer settings, these may or may not print out with the data.

**1** *Click the File menu.*

**2** *Click Page Setup.*

**3** *Click the Sheet tab.*

**4** *Click to place or remove the tick in the Gridlines box.*

## 5.6 | Headers and Footers

**Assessment Objective 5c**

You can add information above or below a chart or spreadsheet by inserting it into the top margin (a header) or bottom margin (a footer) of a worksheet.

As well as your own text, you can insert or format an automatic entry:

**1** Format text.

**2** Page number.

**3** Number of pages.

**4** Date.

**5** Time.

**6** File name and pathway.

**7** File name.

**8** Sheet name.

**9** Picture from file.

**10** Format picture.

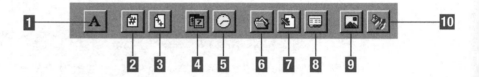

## 5.6.1 Creating Headers and Footers

1 *Click the View menu.*

2 *Click Header and Footer.*

Or

3 *Click the File menu.*

4 *Click Page Setup.*

5 *Click the Header/Footer tab.*

6 *Click Custom Header.*

7 *Click in one of the three sections.*

8 *Enter the text you require*

Or

9 *Click a toolbar button to insert an automatic entry.*

10 *Click OK.*

11 *Repeat for a Custom Footer.*

12 *Click OK.*

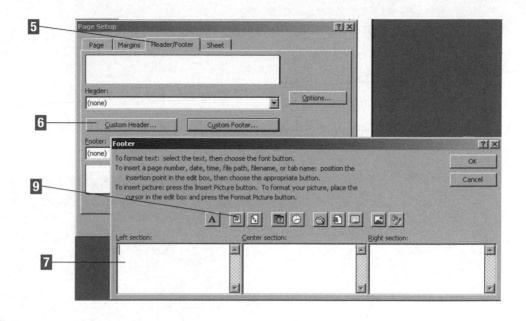

## 5.7 Printing

### 5.7.1 Printing Using Default Settings

Assessment Objective 5d

If you click the Print toolbar button, you will print out the active worksheet showing just a chart on its own page or the data that has been entered.

### 5.7.2 Making Changes

To control what you print you must select different settings. The choices include:

- Fitting a wide or large spreadsheet onto fewer pages.
- Displaying row and column headings on the printout.
- Printing the underlying formulae.
- Printing different parts of a workbook or sheet.
- Printing different numbers of copies.
- Printing charts or graphs alone or with the related data.

 **Critical Error**
**Missing printouts.**

## 5.7.3  Fitting a Spreadsheet onto One Page

1  *Click the File menu.*

2  *Click Page Setup.*

3  *Click the Page tab.*

**4**  *Click in the radio button to reduce the font size of your spreadsheet so that all the data fits on one page.*

## 5.7.4  Displaying Spreadsheet Row and Column Headings

**Assessment Objective 5e**

1  *Click the Sheet tab.*

**2**  *Click in the box to print row and column headings.*

3  *On the printout, this means that together with the data, you will see column letters A, B, C etc. and row numbers 1, 2, 3 etc. in grey boxes.*

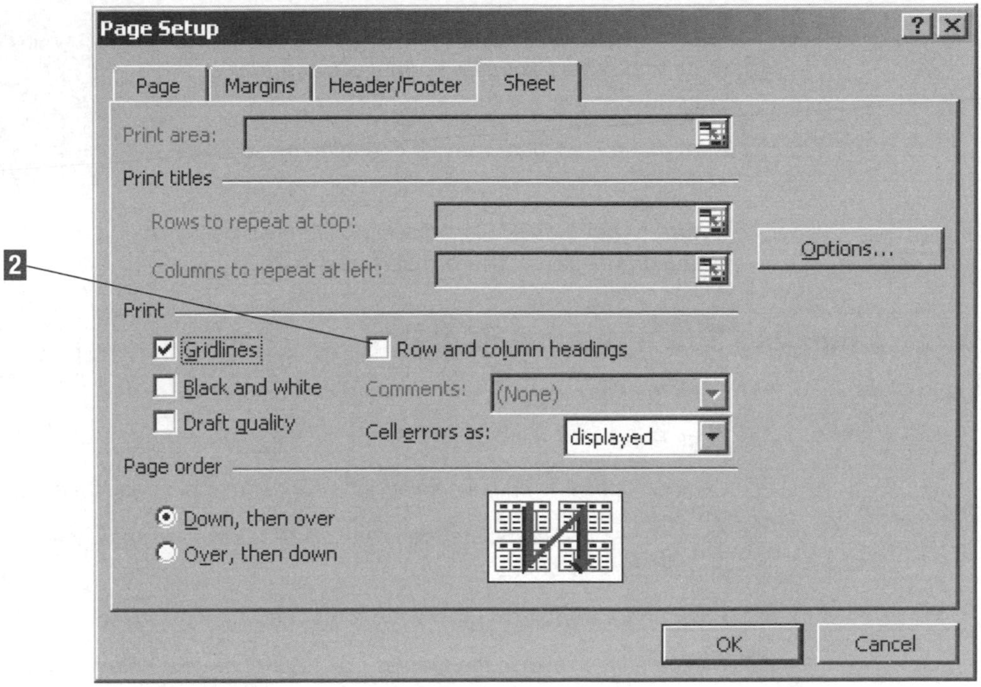

Page Setup dialog box showing the Sheet tab with Print area, Print titles (Rows to repeat at top, Columns to repeat at left), Print options (Gridlines checked, Black and white, Draft quality, Row and column headings, Comments (None), Cell errors as displayed), Page order (Down, then over selected; Over, then down), Options button, OK and Cancel buttons. Label 2 points to the Row and column headings checkbox.

## 5.7.5 Showing Underlying Formulae

**Assessment Objective 5e**

When spreadsheets print out, you normally display the results of any calculations. To see how these were performed, you can view and print the underlying formulae. In this mode, columns will usually increase in width.

| | A | B | C | D |
|---|---|---|---|---|
| 1 | Item | Number sold | Cost per item | Total Cost |
| 2 | Writing pad | 22 | 6.5 | =B2*C2 |
| 3 | Notebook | 14 | 3 | =B3*C3 |
| 4 | Sketch pad | 17 | 7.45 | =B4*C4 |
| 5 | Box of pencils | 3 | 9.5 | =B5*C5 |
| 6 | Box of crayons | 7 | 11.5 | =B6*C6 |
| 7 | TOTAL | | | =SUM(D2:D6) |
| 8 | AVERAGE PRICE | | =AVERAGE(C2:C6) | |

1  *View the spreadsheet on screen.*

2  *Hold **Ctrl** and press the key marked ¬ (next to no. 1).*

Or

3  *Click Tools.*

4  *Click Options.*

5. Click the View tab.

6. Click to place a tick in the Formulas box under Window options.

7. Print the spreadsheet without changing these settings.

8. Return to normal view by pressing Ctrl plus ¬ again or taking off the tick in the Formulas box.

## 5.7.6 Changing Settings in the Print Box

1. Click the File menu.

2. Click Print.

3. Click Selection if you have selected a subset of the spreadsheet data.

4. Click Pages and complete the From: and To: boxes to specify which pages of a large spreadsheet to print.

5. Click Entire workbook if you want to print all the worksheets it contains.

6. Click the up arrows in the Copies box to print more than one copy.

7. Click OK to complete the print.

## 5.7.7 Printing Charts and Graphs on a Separate Sheet

Assessment
Objective 5f

When creating a chart or graph using the Chart Wizard, you can specify that it is created on its own sheet at Step 4. To print that sheet, open it on screen before clicking the Print button.

## 5.7.8 Printing Charts that are on the Same Sheet as the Data

**1** *Click the chart or graph before printing and it will print alone. It will display a black border.*

**2** *Do not click it and both data and chart will print together.*

**3** *Check in Print Preview to make sure you are printing correctly.*

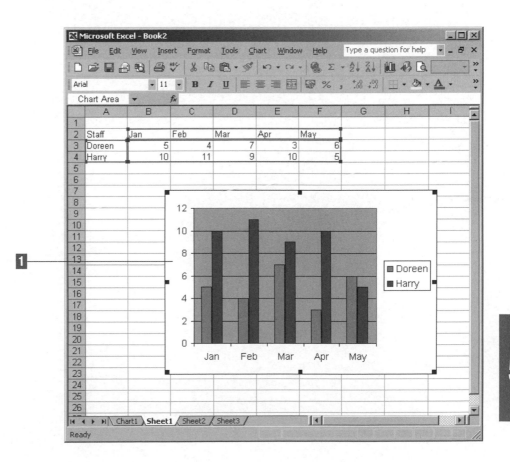

FILE MANAGEMENT AND
E-DOCUMENT PRODUCTION

1

CREATING SPREADSHEETS
AND GRAPHS

2

# DATABASE MANIPULATION

3

PRODUCING AN E-PUBLICATION

4

CREATING AN E-PRESENTATION

5

E-IMAGE CREATION

6

WEB PAGE CREATION

7

ONLINE COMMUNICATION

8

## Learning outcomes

At the end of this unit, you should be able to:

→ Identify and use database software correctly

→ Enter data in an existing database and present and print database files

→ Create simple queries/searches on one or two criteria and sort data

→ Produce appropriate pre-defined reports from databases using short cuts

→ Present data in full

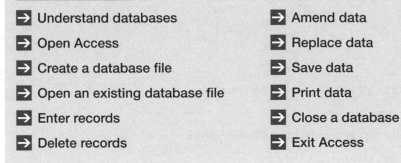

# Database Records

CHAPTER 1

1

## What You'll Do

→ Understand databases

→ Open Access

→ Create a database file

→ Open an existing database file

→ Enter records

→ Delete records

→ Amend data

→ Replace data

→ Save data

→ Print data

→ Close a database

→ Exit Access

## 1.1 What are Databases?

You can keep computerised details of people, objects, events etc. in various places such as spreadsheets or word processed tables. These are all databases, as the data is organised under headings and is set out in such a way that it is very easy to read, sort and search for information.

Applications such as Microsoft Access are known as database management programs and they allow you not only to set up tables of data but to do much more with them. You can enter data using a form rather than directly into the table, you can link and search across several tables and you can create reports that present the data in a professional and attractive way.

## 1.2 The Structure of a Database Table

Imagine that you want to keep details of all your friends. You could organise this under various headings such as First Name, Surname, House number, Road, Town, Postcode, Telephone number, Email address etc. Each heading in a database is known as a **field name** with the data included in that category known as a **field**.

Information about each friend entered under all the headings makes up a complete **record**.

Field
name

| First name | Surname | Email | Age | Town |
|---|---|---|---|---|
| Harry | Spalding | hspald@hotmail.com | 24 | London |
| Moire | Hatton | Hatton_m@compuserve.com | 28 | Woking |
| Sally | French | s.french1@sparkling.co.uk | 34 | London |

Record

Field

## 1.2.1  Data Types

Each field will allow only one type of entry. This could be:

- Text, e.g. a surname or town.
- Number, e.g. their age or number of brothers or sisters.
- Date, e.g. their birthday.
- Currency, e.g. their salary.
- Yes or no, e.g. do they smoke or not?
- AutoNumber, e.g. every new record in the database could be numbered sequentially.
- Memo, e.g. if you want to include a wordy description of them.

These are set when the table is designed. Access can then match text entries and recognise numeric fields so that calculations can be performed when you search for specific records.

## 1.3  Creating a Database

### 1.3.1  Opening Access

[1] *Click the Start button.*

[2] *Click All Programs.*

[3] *Click Microsoft Access.*

Or

[4] *Click a shortcut icon if one is present on the desktop* 🖼.

### 1.3.2  Creating a Database File

When Access opens, there is no blank page to work on. Instead, you must create the file before you can set up tables and add records. The File New Database window looks just like the Save As window you see when using other Microsoft applications.

**1** *Click the File menu.*

**2** *Click New.*

Or

**3** *Click the New toolbar button.*

**4** *On the New File Task pane that will open, click Blank Database.*

**5** *Enter the name for your new file into the File name: box.*

**6** *Select a suitable location to save the file.*

**7** *Click Create.*

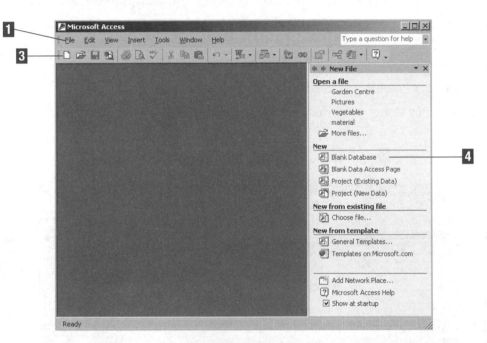

## 1.3.3  Parts of a Database File

When the file opens, you see a restored database window. Leave this rather than maximising it as you will need it only in order to select the objects to work with.

The database window displays a variety of tabs and buttons. You will need to work with the following parts of the window for New CLAIT:

**1** Tables tab – the default opening tab where you create and store tables of data.

**2** Queries tab – go here to create search objects when you want to find specific records.

**3** Forms tab – displays objects used for entering records into the table.

**4** Reports tab – displays objects created for presenting data based on specific records.

**5** Open button – click this to view the records in the table or query, or to preview a form or report.

**6** Design view button – click this to look at the underlying structure of any object.

**7** New button – click this to create an object automatically.

**8** Close button – click this to close the file.

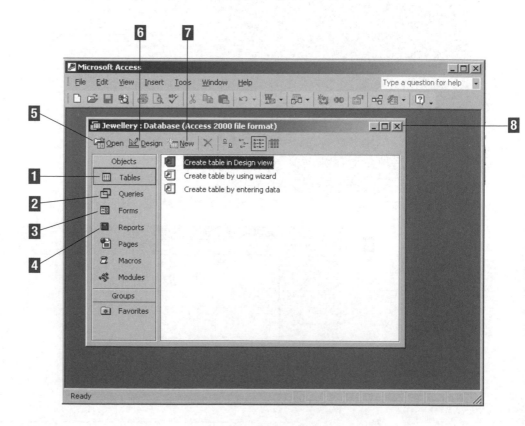

## 1.4 Database Tables

### 1.4.1 Designing a Database Table

You must have a table set up before you can add any records. Although this is not required for New CLAIT, it is a good idea to understand how tables are designed. There are different methods available, but this section will show you how tables are designed in Design view.

[1] *Click the link on the Tables tab to Create Table in Design view.*

[2] *When the window opens, type a field name into the first empty cell in the Field Name column.*

[3] *Press the Tab key or click with the mouse in the next column to select a data type. Text appears as the default but to select a different one:*

[A] *Click the drop down arrow in the box and select from the list.*

[B] *Start typing a data type and it will appear automatically.*

[4] *If there are any instructions or comments the table designer needs to add, these can be typed into the Description column.*

[5] *Click the next Field Name cell and type the name for the next field in the table.*

[6] *Continue entering field names and setting data types until the table design is complete.*

## 1.4.2 Field Properties

For any field, a Properties box below the field name list shows the settings that will be applied. These can all be amended. They include:

- Field size – the space left for characters entered into the field, or the type of number displayed. Long Integer suppresses decimals but Double lets them appear.

- Format – the appearance of numbers, currency, dates etc. Dates can be Long (12th April 2007), Medium (12–Apr–07) or Short (12/4/07).

- Decimals – the number of decimal places displayed.

- Validation Rule – this prevents the wrong data being entered.

- Index – some fields can be indexed for quicker searches.

## 1.4.3 Saving a Table

After designing or amending a table design, it must be saved before you can close it or enter records.

**1** *Click the Save button on the toolbar.*

**2** *You could also click the Datasheet button if you want to start entering records.*

**3** *Click the Close button to close the table and return to the database window.*

**4** *Whichever choice you have made, a Save As box will open if the table has not yet been saved.*

**5** *Enter a name for the table. Make this different from the database file name.*

**6** *Click OK.*

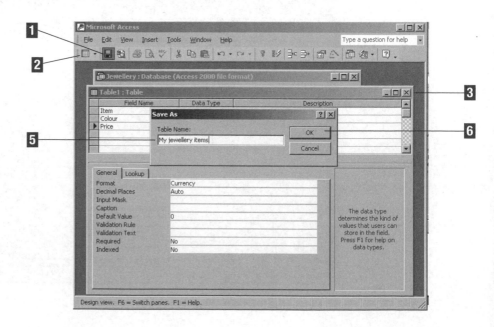

### 1.4.4 Primary Key

Every record in a professional database should have one field that contains unique data, preventing confusion with other, similar records. This might be an individual's NHS or National Insurance number, a stock code, a book ISBN or a booking number etc. The field with such unique identifiers is known as the primary key field. A primary key is also necessary if you want to link more than one table.

When a table is saved, a warning is displayed if a primary key has not been set.

1. Click No if you do not want to set a primary key. (For New CLAIT, no table will have a primary key.)

2. Click Yes to let Access set one by adding a new I.D. field.

3. Click Cancel to assign a primary key manually to the most suitable field.

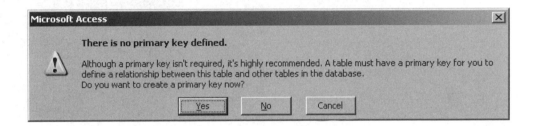

### 1.4.5 Setting a UK Date

If you find dates automatically appearing with the month in front of the day, for example 12/23/07, you must change your computer's Regional settings to set a UK date.

1. Click the Start button.

2. Click Control Panel.

3. Double click Regional and Language Options.

4. On the Regional Options tab, click in the Select an item box and make sure English (United Kingdom) is set.

5. Click OK.

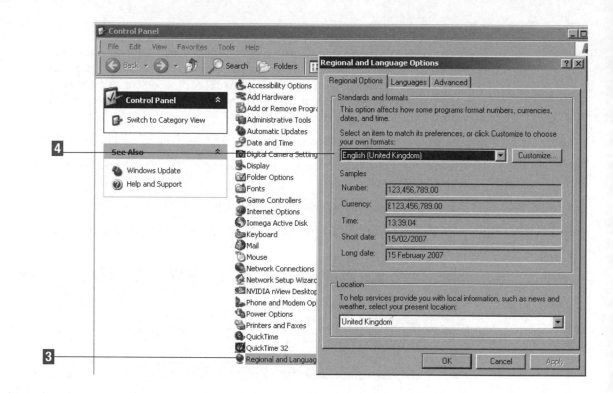

## 1.5 Locating the Records

### 1.5.1 Opening a Database

**Assessment Objective 1a**

Find a database file stored on your computer or a drive in one of the following ways:

**1** *Open the New File Task pane.*

**2** *Click a named database showing in the window.*

**3** *Click More files to browse through files on your computer.*

Or

**4** *Click the File menu.*

**5** *Click Open.*

Or

**6** *Click the Open toolbar button.*

**7** *Browse through the files showing in the Open window.*

**8** *Click the file.*

**9** *Click Open or Press Enter.*

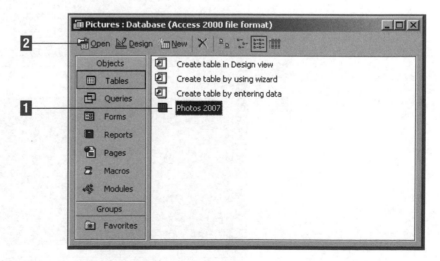

**Critical Error**
Not opening and using the database provided.

## 1.5.2 Opening a Table

The named table will be visible on the database window. Open it in one of two ways:

**1** *Double click the name*.

**2** *Click to select it and click the Open button*.

Opening a table

## 1.6 Entering Records

**Assessment Objective 1b**

Once a table has been designed, you can enter records into the table or use a form to add new data.

### 1.6.1 Using the Table

When a table is open (Datasheet view), you will see columns labelled with the field names.

1. *Click into the first empty field name cell to start entering a new record.*

2. *You must always start a new record on the first empty row. This is marked by an \* in the row selector box.*

3. *The current record is shown by a pencil symbol.*

4. *Work from left to right across the row, not down columns.*

5. *Move from cell to cell by pressing the Tab or arrow key or clicking the mouse.*

6. *Where currency or number data types have been set, tab to the cell so that you can type over the zeros that will be displayed.*

7. *Enter any style of number or date/time, the field properties will determine how the entry is actually displayed.*

**Yes or No?**

Some Yes/No fields display a box rather than text. Click in the box to add a tick for Yes and leave blank for No.

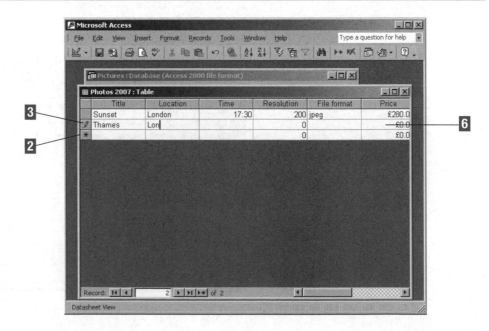

## 1.6.2 Using a Form

Some styles of form look like tables, but a common style is Columnar, with each record displayed on its own.

**1** *Click the New Record selector button to move to the next empty record.*

**2** *Use the Tab key to move from field to field before entering the data.*

**3** *Click the Next Record button to add the next record.*

| Photos 2007 | | _ □ × |
|---|---|---|
| Title | Thames | |
| Location | London | |
| Time | | 13:00 |
| Resolution | | 300 |
| File format | jp | |
| Price | | £0.00 |

Record: 14 ◄ 2 ► ►I ►✱ of 2

**3** **1**

Always use consistent upper or lower case when entering or amending data, and take care not to duplicate records by mistake.

## 1.6.3 Checking

A database is no use if the information it contains is inaccurate. Always check entries manually, as well as using the spell checker.

1. Click the Spelling button to start checking through a table or form.

2. For a highlighted entry, click Ignore if it is accurate.

3. Click an alternative in the Suggestions box and click Change to update the table.

4. Click into the word and amend manually if there are no suitable suggestions, before clicking Change.

5. Click Add to add the word to the built-in dictionary.

6. Click Cancel to stop spell checking.

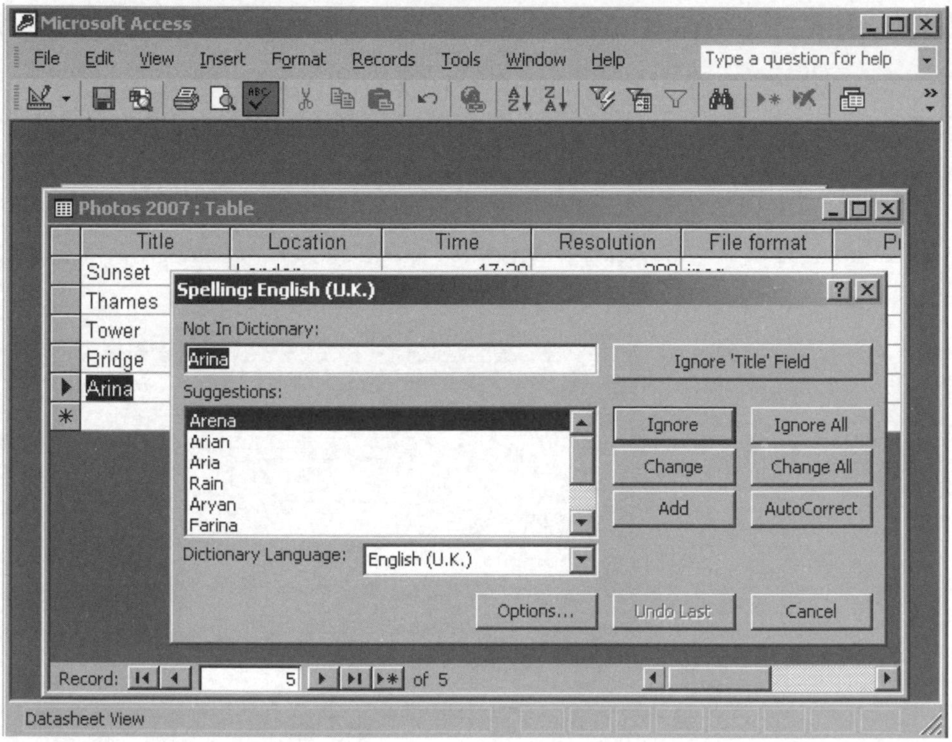

## 1.7 Deleting Records

**Assessment Objective 1c**

When removing an entire record, you will see a warning as, once deleted, you cannot use Undo to restore it again.

### 1.7.1 Deleting a Record

**1** *Click the row selector box to select an entire record.*

**2** *Press the Delete key.*

Or

**3** *Click the Delete button on the toolbar.*

**4** *Click Yes to confirm the deletion.*

## 1.8 Amending Data

**Assessment Objective 1d**

When you need to make any changes, either replace the entire entry or just add or delete characters.

### 1.8.1 Changing Records

[1] *Use an arrow or the Tab key to move to a field entry. The entire entry will be selected.*

[2] *Start typing to replace the entry.*

[3] *Click in a cell to amend part of an entry.*

Or

[4] *Press function key F2 to place the cursor inside the cell.*

| Photos 2007 : Table | | | | | |
|---|---|---|---|---|---|
| Title | Location | Time | Resolution | File format | Price |
| Sunset | London | 17:30 | 200 | jpeg | £280.00 |
| Thames | London | 13:00 | 300 | jpeg | £150.00 |
| Tower | Pisa | 14:30 | 300 | PNG | £300.00 |
| Bridge | Florence | 11:00 | 200 | PNG | £155.00 |
| * | | | 0 | | £0.00 |

## Warning

Only make changes to the data that are specified.

# 1.9 Replacing Data

Assessment Objective 1e

When replacing repeated entries with the same word, or locating an entry in a large database that must be replaced, use the find and replace tools available with all Microsoft Office applications.

## 1.9.1 Using Find and Replace

1. *Click the Edit menu.*

2. *Click Replace.*

Or

3. *Click the Replace tab in the Find box.*

4. *Enter the original database entry in the Find What: box.*

5. *Enter the replacement in the Replace With: box.*

6. *The Look In: box will display the field that will be searched. This is the field marked by your cursor. If it is not the correct field, click the drop down arrow and select the named table to search all entries.*

7. *Click the drop down arrow in the Match: box if you want to search for part of a field, or the start, rather than find a complete entry.*

8. Click in the Search box to change the direction of the search if you are already nearer the bottom of a table.

9. *If you are sure all criteria have been set correctly, click Replace All.*

10. *To check by eye, click Find Next. When an entry is highlighted, click Replace to change it or Find Next to move on to the next match.*

Photos 2007 : Table

| | Title | Location | Time | Resolution | File format | Pri |
|---|---|---|---|---|---|---|
| ▶ | Sunset | London | 17:30 | 200 | jpeg | |
| | Thames | London | 13:00 | 300 | jpeg | |
| | Tower | Pisa | 14:30 | 300 | PNG | |
| | Bridge | Florence | 11:00 | 200 | PNG | |

**Find and Replace**

| Find | Replace |
|---|---|

**4** → Find What: London ▼ — Find Next → **10**

**5** → Replace With: LND ▼ — Cancel

**6** → Look In: Photos 2007 : Table ▼ — Replace

**7** → Match: Whole Field ▼ — Replace All → **9**

Search: Any Part of Field / Whole Field / Start of Field — Search Fields As Formatted

## 1.10 Saving Data

### 1.10.1 Automatic Saves

**Assessment Objective 1f**

You will notice that after entering new records, these are saved automatically and you will not be asked if you want to save them.

### 1.10.2 When to Save

If you change entries, work on the table layout or create a new object, you will be asked to save.

1 Click the Save button.

2 If saving for the first time, enter a name in the Save As: box.

3 Click OK.

## 1.11 Printing Data

**Assessment Objective 1g**

The default print setting for printing a table is portrait orientation. As database tables can contain a number of fields, the paper is often not wide enough to display all the entries on one page. You must also ensure that columns display data in full and that field names print out with the records.

**Critical Error**
Missing printouts.

## 1.11.1 Checking Before Printing

1. Click the File menu.

2. Click Print Preview to check what the printout will look like.

3. Click Setup to open the settings box and change orientation if necessary.

4. The table name and date will be added automatically as a header.

5. Click the Print button to print from Print Preview.

## 1.11.2 Changing Orientation

1. Click the File menu.

2. Click Page Setup.

3. Click the Page tab.

4. Click in the Landscape Orientation radio button.

5. Click OK.

## 1.11.3 Printing Headings

1. Click the File menu.

2. Click Page Setup.

3. Click the Margins tab.

4. Click to place a tick in the Print Headings box.

## 1.11.4 Displaying Data in Full

1. Move the pointer up to the field name.

2. Position the pointer over the right hand boundary.

3. When it shows a two-way arrow, click and hold down the mouse button.

4. Gently drag the boundary to the right to widen the column.

Or

5. Double click the mouse button to widen the column to fit the longest entry exactly.

**Planting : Table**

| | Name | Ideal month | Type | Number planted | Date |
|---|---|---|---|---|---|
| | Spring onio | February | Salad | 35 | 12-Feb-07 |
| ▶ | Carrot | March | Root veg | 50 | 04-Mar-07 |
| | Parsley | February | Herb | 20 | 11-Mar-07 |
| | Lettuce | March | Salad | 40 | 03-Apr-07 |
| | Broccoli | March | Leafy veg | 25 | 12-Apr-07 |
| | Leek | March | Root veg | 40 | 18-Apr-07 |
| | Tomatoes | May | Salad | 65 | 10-May-07 |
| | Beetroot | May | Root veg | 15 | 16-May-07 |
| | Courgette | June | Salad | 30 | 02-Jun-07 |
| | Runner bea | June | Legume | 15 | 18-Jun-07 |
| * | | | | 0 | |

## 1.11.5 Printing

1. Click the Print button on the toolbar for one copy of a database table using the default settings.

2. Click the File menu.

3. Click Print to change settings.

4. Click Selected Record to print a single record.

5. Click Pages and enter page numbers to print a selected range of pages.

6. Change the entry in the Copies box to print more than one copy.

7. Click OK to print.

Print dialog box:

**Print** ? X

**Printer**
Name: Brother MFC-5440CN Printer ▼ Properties

Status: Ready
Type: Brother MFC-5440CN Printer
Where: BRN_731FB1
Comment: BRN_731FB1 ☐ Print to File

**5**

**Print Range**
○ All
○ Pages From: [ ] To: [ ]
○ Selected Record(s)

**4**

**Copies**
Number of Copies: [1 ⬍]

**6**

☐ Collate

Setup... | OK | Cancel

### Where do I put my personal details?

To add your own details such as your name and centre number, don't add them as a separate record. Name the table (or query) so that it includes your details, or write them on any printout.

## 1.12    Closing and Exiting

### 1.12.1  Closing a Database

**1** *Click the Close button on the database window.*

Or

**2** *Click the File menu.*

**3** *Click Close.*

## 1.12.2 Exiting Access

[1] *Click the top Close button in the Access window.*

Or

[2] *Click the File menu.*

[3] *Click Exit.*

# CHAPTER 2

# Searching for Data

## What You'll Do

→ Understand searches

→ Use find

→ Create a filter

→ Create a query

→ Sort data

→ Present data

## 2.1 Why Search a Database?

**Assessment Objective 2a**

Databases allow you to find one or more entries or entire records meeting certain criteria. These might be the answers to questions such as:

- What is your uncle's new address and telephone number?

- Do any suitcases cost under £20?

- What are the full details of the CD you bought last April with 'Sunshine' in the title?

- Are there any villa holidays available in Majorca for a family of four?

Searches work by finding entries that *match* the ones you select or type in, as well as those resulting from calculations performed on the data. If you make a mistake and type in an entry that is not identical to those in the underlying table, no records can be displayed.

There are three different ways you can carry out a search:

- *Find* one particular data entry.

- Use a temporary *filter* to remove records that do not meet your criteria.

- Create and save a search object known as a *query* based on your criteria that can be run many times.

Locate a specific field entry using the Find tool.

## 2.2.1 Using Find

1. *Click the Edit menu.*

2. *Click Find.*

3. *Enter your search criterion into the Find What: box.*

4. *Change any settings such as:*

   A. *Searching the whole table rather than a selected field.*

   B. *Searching for part, the start or the whole field entry.*

   C. *Searching Up or Down.*

5. *Click Find Next.*

6. *The first matching entry will be highlighted.*

7. *Click Find Next to find other matches.*

## 2.3 Filters

These work by filtering out any records in a table that do not meet your criteria.

### 2.3.1 Filter by Selection

This type of filter allows you to select all the data in one field and then filter out all records that do not contain a matching entry. You can then view and print the records that are left on screen.

1. *Open the table.*

2. *Click an entry on which to base the search.*

3. *Click the Filter by Selection button.*

Or

4. *Go to the Records menu.*

5. *Click Filter.*

6. *Click Filter by Selection.*

7. *To display all the records again, click Remove Filter.*

## 2.4 Queries

Queries are set up separately from the table and can be saved on the Queries tab so that they can be run again and again. You can use a wizard but it is simpler to design a query yourself.

### 2.4.1 Accepted Criteria

To search a field for matching entries, you must set criteria that Access recognises. These will be in the form of accepted expressions using standard operators. There are a number of expressions you must be able to use for New CLAIT:

| Looking for | Expression |
| --- | --- |
| More than 4 | >4 |
| 4 or more | >=4 |
| Later than 2006 | >31/12/06 |
| Less than £20 | <20 |
| Earlier than 11:00 | <11:00 |
| £16 or less | <=16 |
| Not size 12 | <>12 |
| Not 14th September | <>14/9/07 |
| Between 10 and 100 | Between 10 AND 100<br>Or >10 AND <100 |
| Blue or red | Blue OR Red |
| Equals Paris (exact match) | Paris |
| Number 25 (exact match) | 25 |

### 2.4.2 Designing a Query

1. *Click the Queries tab.*
2. *Double click Create query in Design view.*
3. *Click the table you want to search.*
4. *Click Add to add it to the Query window.*
5. *Click Close to close the Show Table window.*

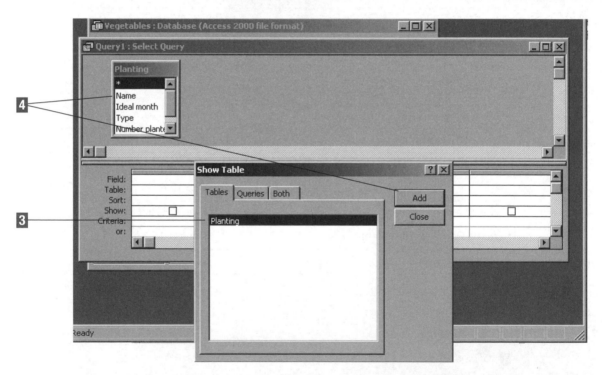

**Does it matter if I have the same two tables showing in the window?**

It is easy to click Add twice by mistake, but you do not want duplicate tables. If you have added the same table twice, select the duplicate by clicking on its border and then press Delete to remove it from the window.

## 2.4.3  Adding Field Names

**1** *Select the first field you want to view or search and add it to the lower query grid.  There are several ways to do this:*

**A** *Double click its name in the field list.*

**B** *Click it, hold down the mouse button and drag it onto the grid.*

**C** *Click in a Field Name cell and select the field from the drop down list.*

**2** *Each new field should be added to the top of the next column.*

**3** *Leave out any fields you do not want to view when the search is complete.*

## 2.4.4  Entering Search Criteria

**1** *For any field that will be searched for matching entries, enter the appropriate expression into its Criteria row.*

**2** *Click in another column or press Tab to move away and accept the expression.*

**A** *Text entries will now display quote marks and may have the word Like added.*

**B** *Date/time entries will display # symbols.*

**C** *No change will be made to numerical entries.*

**3** *Click the Run button to view matching records.*

Or

**4** *Click the Datasheet button.*

**5** *To save the query for future use, click the Save button.*

6 *Enter a name in the Save As box.*

7 *Click OK.*

8 *Close the query and its name will be visible on the Query tab in the database window.*

### Take care when entering criteria!

Note that you will not be offered any entries to select from but must type them yourself. If you do not enter the data correctly, Access will not be able to find an exact match.

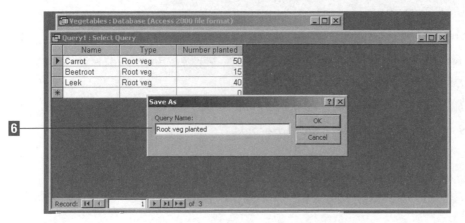

## 2.5 Searching on Two or More Criteria

### 2.5.1 Filter by Form

Assessment
Objective 2b

Filter by Selection can only display records matching a single criterion. To search for records matching two or more criteria, use Filter by Form.

1. *Click the Filter by Form button* 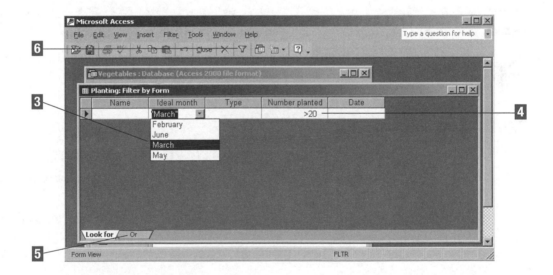*.*

2. *When the empty grid appears, delete any entries if they have been left over from a previous search.*

3. *Click in any field and select an entry from the drop down list.*

4. *To perform calculations, click in the field and enter an accepted expression.*

5. *For either/or, enter one match, click the Or tab at the bottom of the screen and select another match in a different or the same field.*

6. *Click the Apply Filter button to see matching records.*

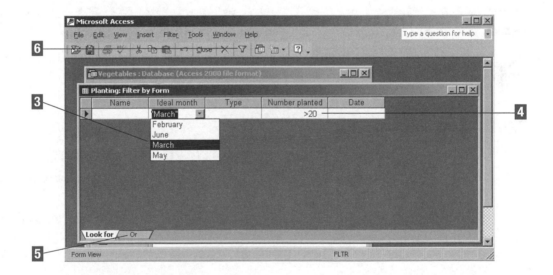

### 2.5.2 Using a Query

1. *Design a query as described earlier.*

2. *Enter expressions in the Criteria row for any fields on which you want to base the search.*

3. *Run the query to see matching records.*

4. *Name and save the query.*

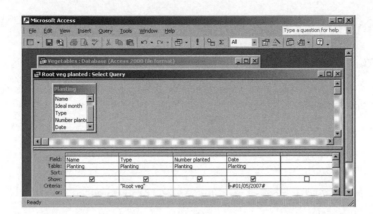

> ## ⊗ Critical Error
> An incorrect search result due to the use of the wrong criteria.

## 2.6 Sorting Data

Assessment Objective 2c

You cannot enter records between those already present. Instead, use a sort to change the order of your records. You can then sort them alphabetically by Name, in descending order of Price, from the earliest to the latest Date etc.

### 2.6.1 Sorting in a Query

1. *Click in the Sort row for any field on which to base the sort.*

2. *Click Ascending for an alphabetical sort, or from the lowest/smallest to the highest/largest entry.*

3. *Click Descending for a sort from largest to smallest or a reverse alphabetical sort.*

4. *Run the query as normal.*

## 2.6.2 Sorting a Table

1 *Click any entry in the field on which you want to base the sort.*

2 *Click the A–Z button for an ascending sort.*

3 *Click the Z–A button for a descending sort.*

2

2 3

**Microsoft Access**

File  Edit  View  Insert  Format  Records  Tools  Window  Help  Type a question for help

**Planting : Table**

| Name | Ideal month | Type | Number planted | Date |
|------|-------------|------|----------------|------|
| Spring onion | February | Salad | 35 | 12-Feb-07 |
| Carrot | March | Root veg | 50 | 04-Mar-07 |
| Parsley | February | Herb | 20 | 11-Mar-07 |
| Lettuce | March | Salad | 40 | 03-Apr-07 |
| Broccoli | March | Leafy veg | 25 | 12-Apr-07 |
| Leek | March | Root veg | 40 | 18-Apr-07 |
| Tomatoes | May | Salad | 65 | 10-May-07 |
| Beetroot | May | Root veg | 15 | 16-May-07 |
| Courgette | June | Salad | 30 | 02-Jun-07 |
| Runner bean | June | Legume | 15 | 18-Jun-07 |
| * | | | 0 | |

Record: 1 of 10

Datasheet View

**Critical Error**
Data losing its integrity as records are split, which can happen if you use an application such as spreadsheet software that allows single column sorting.

## 2.7 Presenting Selected Fields

**Assessment
Objective 2d**

When designing a query you can choose which fields to display and in which order they will appear across the columns.

### 2.7.1 Hiding Fields

You *must* include the search fields in any query, so that criteria can be set. If you do not want to display entries in those fields when the query is run, hide the field on the query grid in Design view.

**1** *When designing a query add the first field you want to see when the query is run. For example, add the Name field.*

**2** *Add subsequent fields, including only those with entries you want to view. For example, Number and Date.*

**3** *Add any search fields, even if you don't want to display their data in the finished query. For example, Type.*

**4** *Enter search criteria for relevant fields.*

**5** *Click off the tick in the Show box for any field you do not want to display when the query is run.*

**6** *In the example the Type field is not visible when the query is run.*

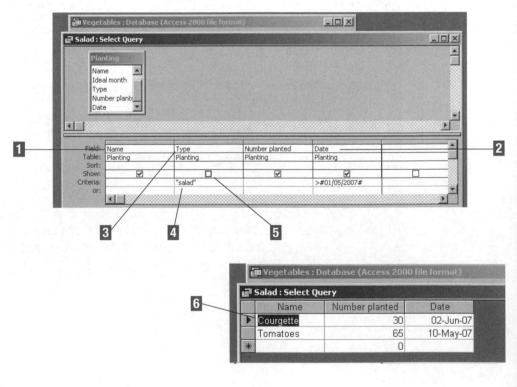

### Does it matter if extra fields are displayed?

Make sure you hide or limit fields on the query grid or you will display too many when the query is printed. For New CLAIT, you must show only the fields specified.

## 2.7.2 Designing a Query Showing All Fields

1. Add all the fields to the grid at the same time by double clicking the asterisk showing at the top of the field list. They will be 'bunched' in the first empty cell in the Field row.

2. Add any fields separately that will be searched.

3. Enter criteria for these fields in the normal way.

4. Take off the tick in the Show box for the added fields so that they will not show when the query is run. (Otherwise, they would appear as duplicate fields, already represented by the full field list added at the start.)

### Is there another way to add all the field names?

If you double click the table name, this selects all the fields. Drag the block of selected fields to the grid and they spread out across the columns. You can now enter search criteria under field names in the normal way.

## 2.8 Printing a Query

Queries are just like tables – print the records after opening or running the query in the same way that you print a table (see page 131, section 1.11).

Save and name the query first, and its name will appear on the printout rather than the default name Query1.

**Critical Error**
Not printing the specified fields.

# CHAPTER 3

# Reports

## What You'll Do

→ Understand reports

→ Produce reports

→ Save reports with a specific name

→ Set page orientation

→ Display data in full

→ Display headers and footers

## 3.1 Understanding Reports

You can print records in table format, but there are limited options when formatting the contents and changing layouts.

For more control over how the final result will appear, you need to create a new object, a report.

## 3.2  Producing Reports

Assessment
Objective 3a

Reports can be based on named tables or queries and can be produced using two different shortcuts: relying on the default settings to create an AutoReport or using a wizard. When using the wizard, click Next to move through the steps.

### 3.2.1  Creating an AutoReport

**1** *Click the Reports tab.*

**2** *Click the New button.*

**3** *Click the style of AutoReport such as Tabular.*

**4** *Click in the box to select the table or query on which to base the report.*

**5** *Click OK.*

**6** *Wait a few seconds for the report to appear.*

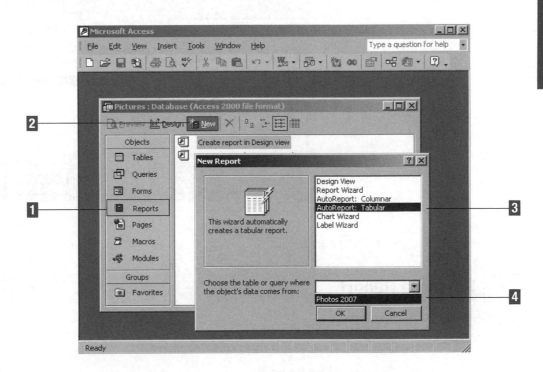

### 3.2.2 Creating a Report Using the Wizard

1. *Double click the link to Create a report using the wizard.*

2. *Click in the box to select the report or query on which to base the report.*

3. *Click each field in turn and then the single arrow button to add it to the report, or click the double arrow to add all fields in their original order.*

4. *Work through the wizard selecting layout and style.*

5. *Some options you do not need for New CLAIT include grouping records under particular fields, sorting the records and adding calculations.*

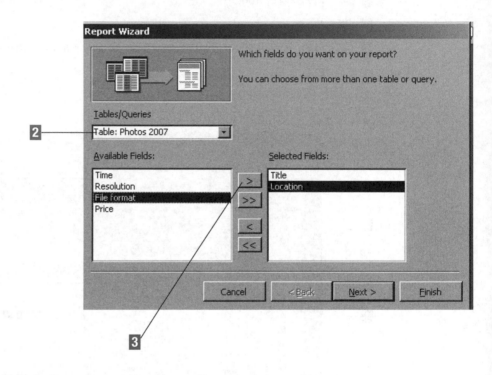

## 3.3 Saving a Report

### 3.3.1 Saving an AutoReport

1. *Click the Save button or try to close the report.*

2. *Click Yes to save the report.*

3. *Enter a suitable name in the Save As box.*

4. *Click OK.*

## 3.3.2 Using the Wizard

1. *At the last step, click in the box to amend the suggested title for the report.*

2. *Click Finish to preview the finished report.*

3. *When the report is closed, it will be saved with the same name as the title.*

## 3.4 Renaming a Report

You may make an error when naming a report (or a table, query or form). You may also want to rename it at some stage.

**1** *Right click the object on the database window.*

**2** *Click Rename.*

**3** *Enter a new name into the box.*

**4** *Click the mouse to accept the change.*

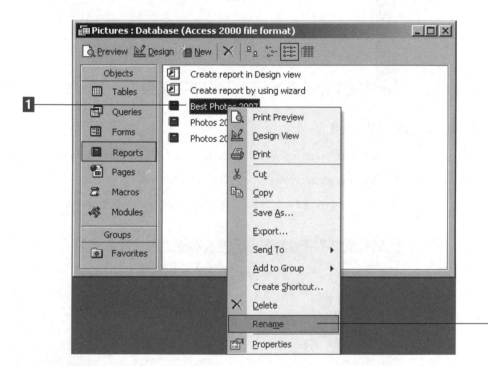

## 3.5 Setting Page Orientation

**Assessment Objective 3b**

An AutoReport is set by default in portrait orientation. You can change this to landscape before printing or set the orientation of a report when creating it using the wizard.

### 3.5.1 Using the Wizard

**1** Go through the steps until you reach the layout page.

**2** Click for Landscape orientation.

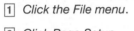

## 3.5.2 Changing Orientation Before Printing

1 *Click the File menu.*

2 *Click Page Setup.*

Or

3 *Click Setup from Print Preview.*

4 *On the Page tab, click in the Landscape radio button.*

5 *Click OK.*

## 3.6 Displaying Data in Full

**Assessment Objective 3c**

Reports often display data poorly – columns can be too close so that entries interfere with each other; column headings may not be positioned over the column entries or labels may not be clear. All these things can be put right by going to the design of the report and making changes to the boxes – controls – containing the entries.

### 3.6.1 Moving and Resizing Controls

1 *Click one box to display small black squares, sizing handles, round the edge.*

2 *Hold Shift as you click other boxes to select more than one. This is useful if you want heading and column data to be amended at the same time.*

**3** *Move the pointer over a box until you see a black hand.*

4 *Drag a box with the pointer and all selected boxes will move together.*

5 *If the pointer shows a single raised finger, dragging will move that box alone.*

6 *Move the pointer over a sizing handle.*

**7** *When it shows a two-way arrow, click and drag to increase or decrease the size of the box.*

8 *Go between Preview and Design view to make sure your amendments have resulted in a better display.*

## 3.7 Headers and Footers

Assessment
Objective 3d

Reports can show two types of entry at the top (header) or bottom (footer) which will either appear automatically or will have to be added:

**1** Entries at the top or bottom of the printed pages are known as page headers and footers.

**2** Entries at the beginning or end of the report are known as report headers and footers.

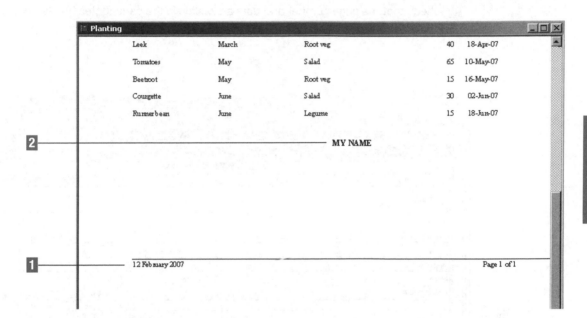

### 3.7.1 Displaying the Header or Footer Area

1 *If a header or footer area is not visible in Design View, move the pointer to the grey bar below the labelled header or footer area.*

2 *Click and drag the bar down to reveal a squared area.*

Or

**3** *Click the View menu.*

**4** *Click to add the relevant header or footer area.*

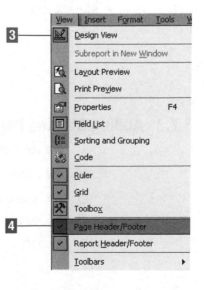

## 3.7.2 Adding Items to the Header or Footer

**1** To add text, click the Label button on the Toolbox.

**2** If the tools are not visible, click the Toolbox button on the toolbar.

**3** Move the pointer into the header or footer area.

**4** Click and drag to draw a box.

**5** Type an entry into the box.

**6** Check that the page number and date are visible in the page footer. You will see codes – today's date (=Now()) and page numbers (="Page" & [Page]).

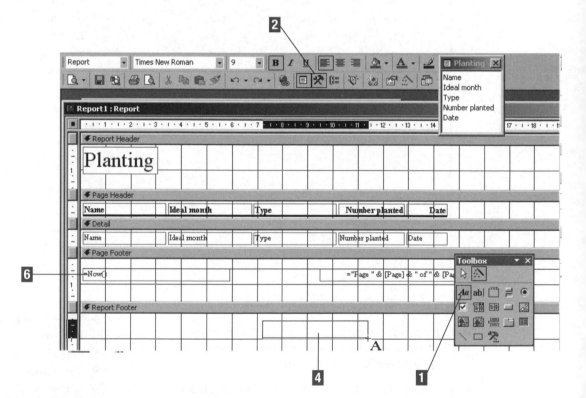

## 3.7.3 Adding Missing Page Numbers or Dates

**1** *Click the Insert menu.*

**2** *Click Page Numbers or Date and Time.*

**3** *Click to add the items.*

**4** *Click for their position.*

**5** *Click OK.*

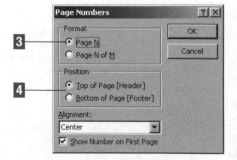

# CHAPTER 1

# Desktop Publishing

1

## What You'll Do

→ Discover desktop publishing

→ Start working with Publisher

→ Set page orientation

→ Amend margins

→ Enter and format text

→ Discover font families

→ Set text columns

## 1.1 What is Desktop Publishing?

When you want to produce professional-looking brochures, leaflets, business cards, invitations or calendars, it is worth using a dedicated application. This will offer a range of publications to customise and will allow you to manipulate and place text and images anywhere on the page. Such programs are known as DTP or desktop publishing applications. There are many commercial applications available, but this chapter uses Microsoft Publisher.

## 1.2 Starting with Publisher

Launch the program from your programs listing or from a desktop icon.

1 *Click the Start button.*

2 *Click All Programs.*

3 *Click Microsoft Publisher.*

Or

4 *Click the Publisher icon if it is visible on the desktop* 🔡.

## 1.3 The Opening Screen

When Publisher opens, there are three main choices of starting point:

**1** *Start from a design – pick a type of publication to customise.*

**2** *Click Blank publication to start with a plain page. This is the correct choice for New CLAIT.*

**3** *Click More publications to browse through your computer files and open an existing file.*

**4** *Once you have started work, open the Task pane from the View menu to return to this starting point.*

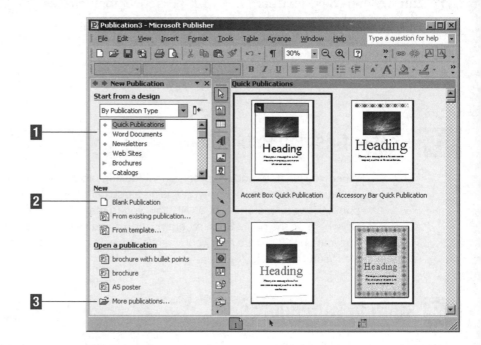

## 1.4 Starting a New Publication

Do this in one of two ways:

**1** *Click the New button.*

Or

**2** *Click the File menu.*

**3** *Click New.*

**4** *Click Blank Publication in the Task pane.*

## 1.5 Opening an Existing Publication

1. *Click the Open button.*

Or

2. *Click the File menu.*

3. *Click Open.*

4. *Browse for the publication.*

5. *Click its name.*

6. *Click Open.*

Or

7. *View the Task pane and select a publication listed under 'Open a publication'.*

## 1.6 The Publisher Screen

When a blank publication opens the screen will display the following items:

1. An empty blank page.

2. The Objects toolbar containing tools for working on your publication.

3. Zoom In (+) and Out (–) buttons to change magnification.

4. Rulers for sizing objects.

5. A display showing which page you are currently working on.

6. Coloured lines showing margins and helping with layout.

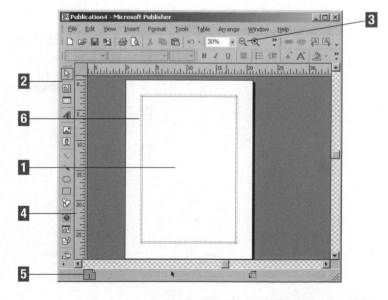

## 1.6.1  Zooming In or Out

You will find that the standard view is at about 30 per cent magnification, which is very low when entering text. Zoom in by:

1. *Pressing the function key F9.*

2. *Clicking the Zoom In button showing a + sign.*

3. *Increasing the measure in the Magnification box.*

Or

4. *Right click the page.*

5. *Click a magnification.*

6. *Reverse the magnification by clicking the Zoom Out button or pressing F9 again.*

## 1.7  Page Orientation

**Assessment Objective 1a**

The default orientation for publications is portrait. Change this to landscape if you want to produce publications with longer sides top and bottom. You can also select a different paper size if you don't want to print a publication on A4 paper.

1. *Click the File menu.*

2. *Click Page Setup.*

3. *Click the Layout tab.*

4. *Click in the Landscape radio button.*

5. *Click in the box for a different size of publication.*

6. *Click OK.*

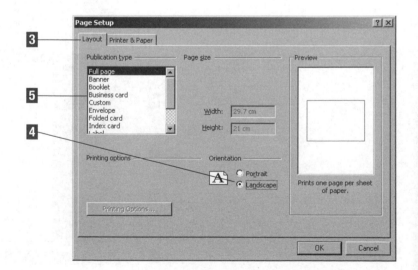

## 1.8 | Margins

**Assessment Objective 1b**

These are set at 2.5 cm by default. For a different width, change settings in the margins box.

1. *Click the Arrange menu.*
2. *Click Layout Guides.*
3. *Change any measures in the left, right, top or bottom margin boxes.*
4. *Click OK.*

### How accurate do margins have to be?

For New CLAIT, make sure margins are within 8 mm (top), 4 mm (bottom) or 6 mm (sides) of the measure you are asked to set.

## 1.9 | Adding Text

**Assessment Objective 1c**

Items in a publication are normally added in a box or frame so that columns of text can be flowed round them. You must draw the box or frame in position on the page before you can start entering your text.

For this unit, you should leave one space after any punctuation.

### 1.9.1 Entering Text

1. *Click the Text Box tool.*
2. *Click and hold down the mouse button on the page. It will show a cross.*
3. *Drag the pointer to draw a box.*
4. *Start typing in the box where the cursor will be flashing.*

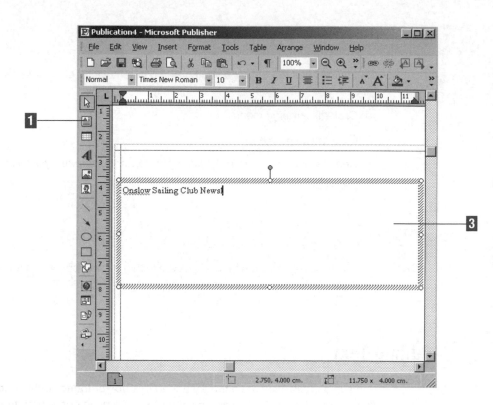

## 1.9.2 Understanding Text Families

**Assessment Objective 1e**

Most Microsoft publications will have a default text font of Arial or Times New Roman.

They belong to two different families of font:

- *Serif* – these have short cross-lines (serifs) at the ends of the characters. Examples include: Times New Roman, Courier New and Bookman Old Style.

- *Sans serif* – these are plainer as they have no short cross-lines. Examples include: Arial, Tahoma and Comic Sans MS.

## 1.10 Formatting Text

Use the normal toolbar buttons or Format – Font menu choices to apply different fonts or add emphasis such as bold or italic to any selected text. These are explained fully in Unit 1.

### Why are my formatting toolbar buttons grey?

In Publisher, you will not be able to access the formatting toolbar until you have clicked the text box.

## 1.10.1 Font Sizes

Assessment
Objective 1f

Your publication may need a heading across the top of the page. You can increase the font size in the normal way or use the Increase Font Size toolbar button that allows you to change the size in steps.

**1** *Select the text you want to format.*

**2** *Click the Increase Font Size button.*

**3** *Keep clicking to increase the font size in steps.*

**4** *Click the Decrease Font Size button to reverse the changes.*

Or

**5** *Click a measure from the drop down list in the Font Size box.*

**6** *If your chosen measure is not offered, type it into the box over the size showing.*

**7** *Press Enter to confirm the font size.*

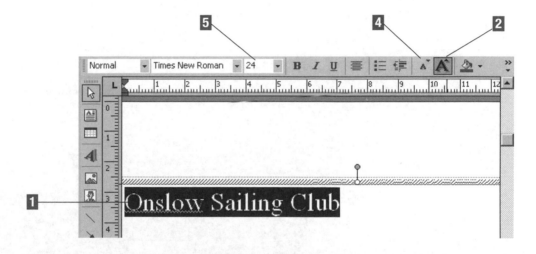

### What sizes should the fonts be?

When setting different font sizes for headings, subheadings and main (body) text, take care to select sizes that differ by *at least* two sizes. For example, select font size 14 (main text), 18 (subheadings) and 24 (heading) rather than 12, 13 and 14.

### Critical Error
Using illegible fonts or font sizes.

## 1.11 Columns

Assessment
Objective 1d Each text box displays a single column of text. If you want your text set out in two or three columns, change the text box properties.

## 1.11.1 Setting Columns

1. *Right click a text box.*

2. *Click Format Text Box.*

3. *Click the Text Box tab.*

4. *Click Columns.*

5. *Increase the number in the Number box.*

6. *Click the arrow in the Spacing box or type in a measure to increase the space between columns.*

7. *Click OK.*

### What is the allowable error?

A 10 per cent tolerance is permitted on spacing between columns.

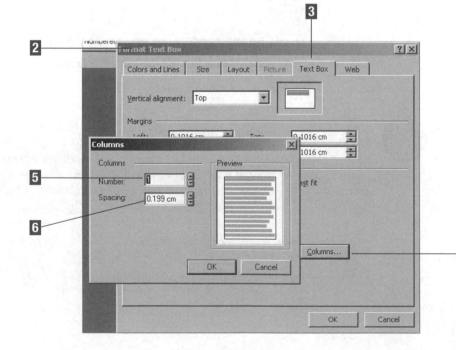

# CHAPTER 2

# Adding Objects

## What You'll Do

→ Import text

→ Import images

→ Use drawing tools

→ Add borders

## 2.1 Importing Text

**Assessment Objective 2a**

Publications are often a collaborative effort, using documents created by colleagues and written elsewhere. Publisher allows you to import text files into your publication. If you have already set columns, the text will flow into these from left to right.

### 2.1.1 Importing a Text File

**1** *Draw a text box on the page.*

**2** *Click the Insert menu.*

**3** *Click Text File.*

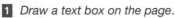

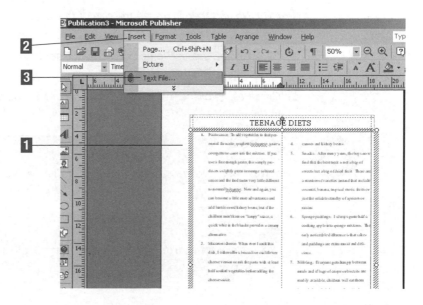

4 *Browse for the file.*

5 *Select the file name and click OK.*

6 *The text will appear on the page inside the frame.*

## 2.1.2  Resizing Frames

When importing long documents, you may not draw a large enough text box. You will see an error message telling you that the text will not fit. Part of the text will be held back and you will see an overflow symbol at the bottom of the text box.

You have three choices:

1 *Click No and then increase the size of the text box to enlarge the space available for the file.*

2 *Click No and select the text on screen. Reduce the font size so that the rest of the document will fit into the box.*

3 *Click Yes. Publisher will create a second or third box, often on another page, in which to fit the rest of the text.*

**Warning**

For New CLAIT, always click No as you must have all the text visible on a single page.

**Critical Error**

Importing the wrong text, an incomplete text or failing to insert the specified text.

**Assessment Objective 2b**

You can add images to your publications and position them within columns of text. The software will then wrap the text round them according to your instructions.

For New CLAIT, a picture will be provided. In your own publications, you may want to insert pictures from the Microsoft Clip Art Gallery. How to do this is explained in Chapter 5.

## 2.2.1 Importing a Picture

**1** *Click the Picture Frame tool.*

**2** *Draw a frame onto the publication. It will push away any text that is under it.*

Or

**3** *Click the Insert menu.*

**4** *Click Picture.*

**5** *Click From File.*

**6** *Browse through your folders to find the specified picture.*

**7** *Select it.*

**8** *Click Insert.*

**9** *The picture will appear on the page.*

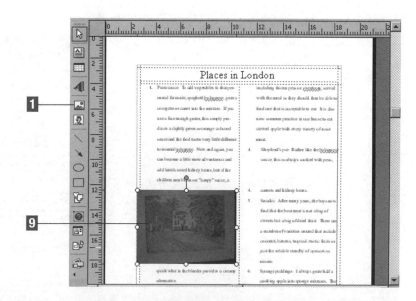

⊗ **Critical Error**
Inserting the wrong image or failing to insert the specified image.

### 2.2.2 Placing Images

Assessment
Objective 2c

When a picture is selected, showing white circular sizing handles round the edge, you can move it into the specified position.

1. *Click the picture if necessary to select it.*

2. *Move the pointer until it displays a van labelled 'MOVE'.*

3. *Drag the picture into position with the mouse.*

Or

4. *Draw a frame on the page before inserting it, so that the picture will be placed correctly.*

## 2.3  Text Flow

Assessment
Objective 2d

There are a number of different ways that you can flow text round a picture which are all examples of *text wrap*. These include:

1. *Square* – text fits neatly round the picture leaving a narrow border.

2. *Tight* – text fits right up to the picture edge.

3. *Top and Bottom* – text wraps above and below the picture, but not on either side.

### 2.3.1  Applying a Text Wrap

1. *Right click the picture.*

2. *Click Picture toolbar.*

Or

3. *Click the Format menu.*

4. *Click Format.*

5. *Click Picture.*

6. *Click the Layout tab.*

7. *Click a text wrap from the options offered.*

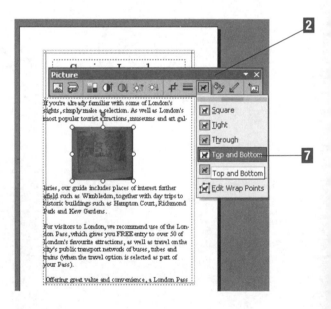

## 2.4 | Lines and Shapes

**Assessment Objective 2e**

Microsoft applications include drawing tools which are available in Publisher from the Objects toolbar. These include:

**1** *Lines.*

**2** *Arrows.*

**3** *Ovals.*

**4** *Rectangles.*

**5** *A range of more complex lines and shapes from the AutoShapes menu.*

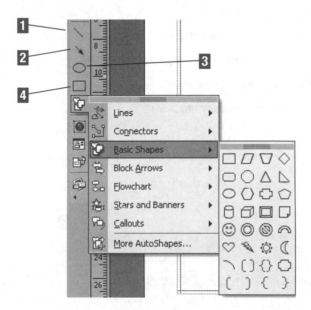

### 2.4.1 Drawing a Shape

**1** *Click a line or shape tool.*

**2** *Move the mouse pointer over the publication. It will show a cross.*

**3** *Click on the publication.*

Or

**4** *Click and hold down the left mouse button.*

**5** *Drag out the shape to your preferred size.*

**6** *Let go and it will be ready for formatting.*

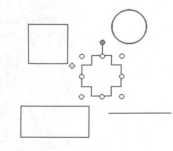

7. To draw a square, hold Shift as you drag out a Rectangle.

8. To draw a circle, hold Shift as you drag out an Oval.

9. To keep a line straight, hold Shift as you draw.

## 2.4.2  Colouring a Shape

1. Click the shape so that it shows white sizing handles.

2. Click the drop down arrow next to the Fill Color button showing a tipping paint pot.

Or

3. Double click the shape to open the Format AutoShape box.

4. Click the Colors and Lines tab.

5. Click the drop down arrow in the Fill Color box.

6. Click a coloured box to fill the shape with that colour.

7. Click No Fill to remove a fill colour.

8. Click More Colors to display the palette.

9. Click any colour.

10. Check the preview to compare the current and new colours.

11. Click OK.

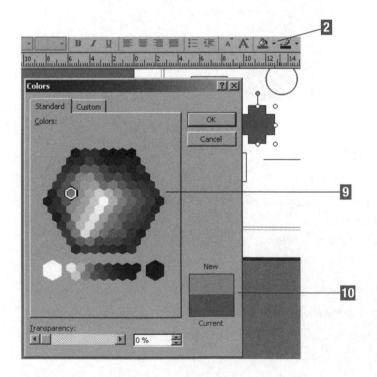

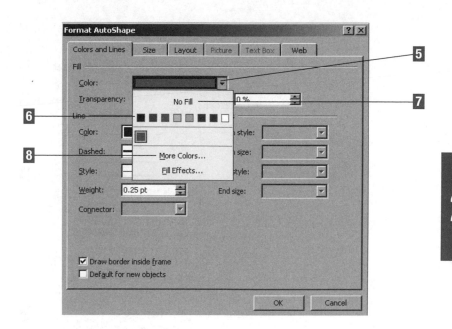

## 2.4.3 Formatting Lines and Borders

Lines and shape or text box borders can be formatted in a number of ways:

- Change style from a solid to a dotted or double line.
- Change to a thicker line by increasing the weight.
- Apply a colour.
- Remove the border altogether.

1 *Click the shape, box or line.*

2 *Click the drop down arrow next to the Line Color button to select a colour.*

3 *Click the Line/Border Styles button.*

4 *Click No Line to remove a line or visible border.*

5 *Click a different line from the display.*

6 *Click More Lines to open the Format AutoShape box.*

Or

7 *Double click the shape.*

8 *Click the Colors and Lines tab.*

9 *Click in the Lines boxes to select style, weight and colour of line.*

10 *Click OK.*

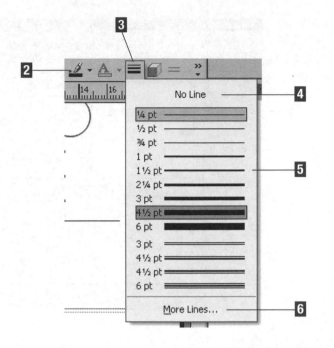

### Can a line be too long?

Make sure that any lines or borders do not extend into the margin or column space.

# Manipulating Text and Images

**CHAPTER 3**

## What You'll Do

→ Align text

→ Amend text

→ Resize headings

→ Check spelling

→ Manipulate images

## 3.1 Text Alignment and Indentation

**3**

**Assessment Objective 3a**

After importing a text file, you must decide how best to display it. Large blocks of text may look better fully justified, so that left and right edges are straight, and you can also indent the paragraphs from the left margin.

List items can be bulleted or numbered to break up the text and columns of text should be balanced at the bottom of the page.

### 3.1.1 Aligning and Indenting Text

1. *Select the text. Use the mouse or click a text box and click Select All on the Edit menu.*

2. *Click one of the alignment buttons on the toolbar:*

    A. *Left.*

    B. *Centre.*

    C. *Right.*

    D. *Justified.*

Or

3. *Right click the text and click Change Text.*

Or

4. *Click the Format menu.*

5. *Click Indents and Lists.*

**6** *Click in the Alignment box to set a different alignment.*

**7** *Click the drop down arrow in the Preset box to set a 1st Line Indent, if you want each paragraph to start in from the left margin, or Hanging Indent to indent all but the first line.*

**8** *Click for a bulleted or numbered list.*

**9** *Click Line Spacing if you want double or 1.5 spacing instead of the default spacing.*

**10** *Click OK.*

| Indents and Lists | ? X |
|---|---|

Indent settings
( • ) Normal    ( ) Bulleted list    ( ) Numbered list — **8**

Indents
Preset: Flush Left
Left:    | Original
         | Flush Left
First line: | 1st Line Indent
         | Hanging Indent
Right:   | Quotation
         | Custom

**7**

Sample

Alignment: Left — **6**

**9** — Line Spacing...    OK    Cancel

## 3.2 Amending Text

Assessment
Objective 3b

New CLAIT requires you to leave text files as they are supplied, apart from correcting spelling mistakes. For your own publications, you may want to move, copy or replace text to improve the content. Use exactly the same methods such as Delete, Cut and Paste or Find/Replace as you would when word processing. These are described fully in Unit 1.

**Critical Error**
Amending the text, for example by changing grammar or word order when it is not specified.

## 3.2.1  Resizing Text

**Assessment Objective 3c**

Your text needs to be balanced at the bottom of the publication, with no more than two lines difference. Do this by slowly increasing the size of the text so that it flows across columns to fill any gaps.

1. *Select the main body text.*

2. *Click the Increase or Decrease Font Size button repeatedly until the text is the correct size.*

3. *Check that headings and subheadings are still different font sizes.*

4. *Check that text is still legible.*

5. *Check that any images are still in the correct place and not obscuring any text.*

6. *Check that the last few words of text are still visible on the page.*

## 3.2.2  Editing a Heading

If a text box is not wide enough to display a heading on a single line:

1. *Click the box to reveal the border.*

2. *Position the pointer over a corner white circle – a sizing handle.*

3. *When it shows an arrow labelled RESIZE, click and hold down the mouse button.*

4. *Drag the border out to increase the size of the box.*

5. *Increase the text to fill the text box by selecting it and then clicking the Increase Font Size button.*

6. To adjust the text by a very small amount:

   A. *Click Format.*

   B. *Click Character Spacing.*

   C. *Adjust the scaling, tracking or kerning to stretch the text slightly.*

**Can a long heading extend over several lines?**

No – do not split headings onto more than one line, or hyphenate any of the words if they are not shown in this way.

Character spacing

### 3.2.3 Moving a Text Box

1. *Move the pointer up to a selected text box border.*
2. *Click and hold down the mouse button when you see a van labelled 'MOVE'.*
3. *Drag the box with the pointer.*

### 3.2.4 Deleting a Text Box

1. *Click the box to select it.*
2. *Press the Delete key.*

Or

3. *Click the Edit menu.*
4. *Click Delete Object.*

## 3.3 Checking Spelling

**Assessment Objective 3d** Proof-read the document manually, in case the spell checker does not pick up misspelt words. Then correct individual words or run the spell checker.

### 3.3.1 Using the Spell Checker

1. *To correct one word: right click the red wavy line and select an alternative, or correct the word manually.*

2. *To check the document: click the Spelling button.*

3. *If an appropriate word is offered in the Change to: box, click Change/Change All.*

4. *Click in the Suggestions box to select an alternative word.*

5. *Correct the word manually if no suggestion is offered.*

6. *Click Change/Change All to update the document.*

7. *Click Ignore/Ignore All to leave a word as it is spelt.*

8. *Click Close to complete or cancel the checking.*

**3**

## 3.4 Manipulating Images

**Assessment Objective 3e**

You will be asked to print your publication twice: once with the picture in one position and then after it has been manipulated. The pictures can be changed in a variety of ways. They can be:

- Moved to a different position.
- Resized.
- Cropped to cut off an unwanted area.
- Flipped or rotated.

### 3.4.1 Moving

1. *Move the mouse pointer over the picture.*
2. *When you see a van labelled 'MOVE', click and hold down the left mouse button.*
3. *Drag the picture to another part of the publication.*

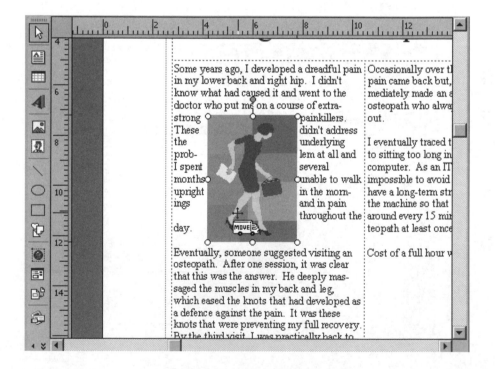

---

### Check the instructions!

It is very easy to misread these and move the picture to the wrong position or to the wrong column.

## 3.4.2 Resizing

1. *Click the picture.*

2. *Position the mouse over a corner sizing handle.*

3. *When you see an arrow labelled 'RESIZE', hold down the mouse button.*

4. *Drag the boundary in or out to resize the picture.*

### My picture looks squashed

Take care to resize pictures from corner sizing handles, so that they maintain their original proportions.

## 3.4.3 Cropping

1. *Right click the picture.*

2. *Click Show Picture Toolbar.*

3. *Click the Cropping tool.*

4. *Click the picture to add a dark dotted outline.*

5. *Position the pointer over a border and drag inwards when you see a T or right angle shape.*

6. *Let go of the mouse and the area outside the dotted line will disappear.*

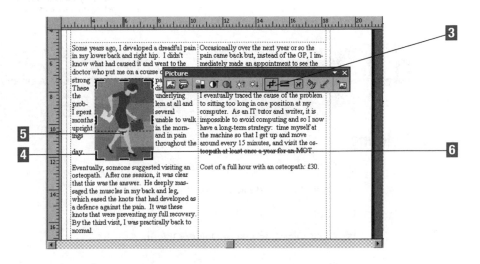

## 3.4.4 Rotating or Flipping

|1| *Click the picture.*

|2| *Position the pointer over the green circle at the end of the rotate arm.*

|3| *When it shows circular arrows, drag the picture round.*

|4| *Hold Shift to rotate in steps of 15°.*

Or

|5| *Click to open the Arrange menu.*

|6| *Click Rotate or Flip.*

|7| *Click one of the options.*

Or

|8| *Right click the picture.*

|9| *Click Format Object.*

|10| *Click the Size tab.*

|11| *Enter an exact measure into the Rotation box.*

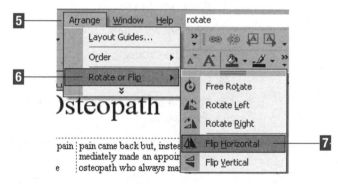

### Warning
**Take care not to carry out any unspecified amendments or allow the image to touch or overlap any text, drawn objects or margins.**

## 3.4.5 Deleting

|1| *Click the picture to select it.*

|2| *Press the Delete key.*

Or

|3| *Right click and select Delete Object.*

# CHAPTER 4

# Saving and Printing a Publication

## What You'll Do

→ Save a publication

→ Add headers and footers

→ Print a publication

→ Close a publication

→ Exit Publisher

## 4.1 | Saving Publications

### 4.1.1 Saving for the First Time

**Assessment Objective 4a**

1. *Click the Save button.*

Or

2. *Click the File menu.*

3. *Click Save.*

4. *Click in the Save In: box to select a suitable location.*

5. *Edit the file name.*

6. *To save the publication as an image or a web page, select a format from the list in the Save as type: box.*

7. *Click Save or press Enter.*

### 4.1.2 Saving Different Versions

1. *Click the File menu.*

2. *Click Save As.*

3. *Give the file a different name and/or select a different location.*

4. *Click Save.*

**I seem to have lost my original publication!**

Make sure you use Save As early, as you must produce evidence of two different versions of your publication, before and after text and images have been manipulated.

## 4.2 Headers and Footers

To add your name, the date or other information into a publication without affecting the layout, either draw a text box at the top or bottom in the margin area or use the Header and Footer facilities.

### 4.2.1 Inserting a Header or Footer

1. *Click the View menu.*

2. *Click Header and Footer.*

3. *Type your text or click an automatic entry for page number, date etc. into the header box.*

4. *Switch to the footer to make an entry here.*

5. *Click Close.*

## 4.3 Printing Publications

**Assessment Objective 4b**

Professional publications are either printed as composites – displaying all the colours in a single printout – or in ways that allow the printer to check the various colours. For New CLAIT Unit 4, use the default settings of your printer as you will not be required to print out in colour.

**Critical Error**
Missing printouts.

### 4.3.1 Printing a Composite Publication

1. *Click the Print button*  *for a single copy of the publication.*

Or

2. *Click the File menu.*

3. *Click Print.*

**Color Printing** ? X

Print all colors as:
- ● Composite RGB
- ○ Process colors (CMYK)
- ○ Spot color(s)
- ○ Single color publication
- ○ Process colors (CMYK) plus Spot color(s)

Selected spot colors:
- Add...
- Modify...
- Delete

Colors to be used in publication:
- ■ Main (Black) -- RGB (0, 0, 0)

Help | OK | Cancel

4 Click in any of the boxes in the Print box to print specific pages or make more than one copy.

5 Click OK.

Hold **Ctrl** and press **P** for a shortcut to printing a single copy.

## 4.4 Closing Publications

Assessment Objective 3b

Each publication will open in its own window. When you close a publication, you will reveal the next open file. After closing the last file, you will be left with Publisher displaying a blank publication.

1 Click the Close button in the top right hand corner.

Or

2 Click the File menu.

3 Click Close.

## 4.5 Exiting Publisher

1. *Click the Close button.*

Or

2. *Click the File menu.*

3. *Click Exit.*

## Learning outcomes

At the end of this unit, you should be able to:

→ Identify and use presentation software correctly

→ Set up a consistent slide layout

→ Select fonts and enter text

→ Import and insert images correctly

→ Use the drawing tools

→ Format slides and presentations

→ Re-order slides and produce printed handouts

→ Manage and print presentation files

# CHAPTER 1

# Using PowerPoint

## What You'll Do

→ Discover presentations

→ Launch PowerPoint

→ Change views

→ Create a new presentation

→ Open an existing presentation

→ Add text

→ Apply a background

→ Exit the application

## 1.1 Why Use PowerPoint?

**Assessment Objective 1a**

Presentation software such as PowerPoint allows you to present information in the form of colourful slides. These can be accompanied by music and can include images, animations or video clips. You can also create documentation such as:

- Copies of the slides.
- Handouts to give to members of the audience.
- Speaker's notes to act as an aide-memoire.
- A text outline of the talk.

## 1.2 Launching PowerPoint

1. *Click the Start button.*

2. *Click All Programs.*

3. *Click Microsoft PowerPoint.*

Or click an icon for the program if one is visible on the desktop.

## 1.3 The Opening Screen

When PowerPoint opens, you will see a window in Normal view. This displays four different panes:

**1** *Slide pane showing a blank title slide.*

**2** *Notes pane where you can type in speaker's notes.*

**3** *Outline/Slides pane showing a text outline of the presentation or thumbnail pictures of the slides. Click the tab to alternate the view.*

**4** *Task pane offering shortcuts to files or various designs and layouts.*

## 1.4 Views

Most work on a presentation will take place on the slide in Normal view and you can expand the area by closing the Task and Outline/Slides panes.

### 1.4.1 Closing a Pane

**1** *Click the Close button at the top of the pane.*

**2** *If it is not visible, increase the width of the pane by dragging out a boundary with the mouse. The pointer will display a two-way arrow.*

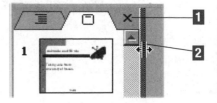

There are a range of views you will want to change to when preparing or running a presentation. Three views are represented by shortcut buttons at the bottom of the Outline/Slides pane:

**1** *Normal* view.

**2** *Slide Sorter* – you will see all the slides in your presentation and can check layouts or change slide order.

**3** *Slide Show* – this runs the presentation. Go to this view to check sounds or timing and the transition from one slide to the next.

Other views are available from the View menu. These are:

■ *Master* – a view in which to add or edit items which will then be displayed throughout the presentation.

■ *Notes Page* – in this view you see the relevant slide and can type your text into a box below it.

■ *Task pane* – reopen this when required.

## 1.4.2 Changing Views

1 *Click the View menu.*

2 *Click the view you want.*

Or

3 *Click one of the view buttons at the bottom of the screen.*

## 1.5 Placeholders

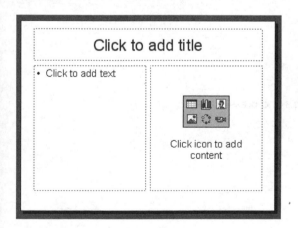

Placeholders

As you build up your presentation you can choose how to arrange text and objects on each slide. To help you, PowerPoint offers various ready-made layouts with areas on the slide set aside for text and/or icons. These areas are known as placeholders. The icons are a shortcut to content such as pictures, charts or video clips.

## 1.6 New Presentations

To start a new presentation, use the Tasks pane or shortcut if it is visible, or the normal menu option.

### 1.6.1 Creating a Presentation

1. *Click the File menu.*

2. *Click New.*

Or

3. *Click Blank Presentation in the Task pane.*

Or

4. *Click the New button on the standard toolbar.*

You can also hold **Ctrl** and press **N**.

## 1.7 Opening an Existing Presentation

1. *Click a named presentation showing in the Task pane.*

2. *Click More presentations to browse through your files.*

Or

3. *Click the File menu.*

4. *Click Open.*

Or

5. *Click the Open toolbar button.*

6. *Select a file listed in the window.*

7. *Click Open.*

A shortcut to the Open box is to hold **Ctrl** and press **O**.

**Adding Text**

**Assessment Objective 1b**

There are two different places to add text: on the Outline tab or straight onto a slide. You can either click into a text placeholder to add your text, or create a new area on the slide.

## 1.8.1 Entering Text on a Slide

**1** *To use a placeholder: click where it instructs you to do so.*

**2** *Start typing. Text size for headings, subheadings etc. will be set by default.*

**3** *In Normal view, the text you type will appear on the Outline tab automatically.*

**4** *To use a text box: click the Text Box tool.*

**5** *Move the pointer over the slide. It will show a cross.*

**6** *Click, hold down the mouse button and draw out the required size of text box.*

**7** *Type into the box.*

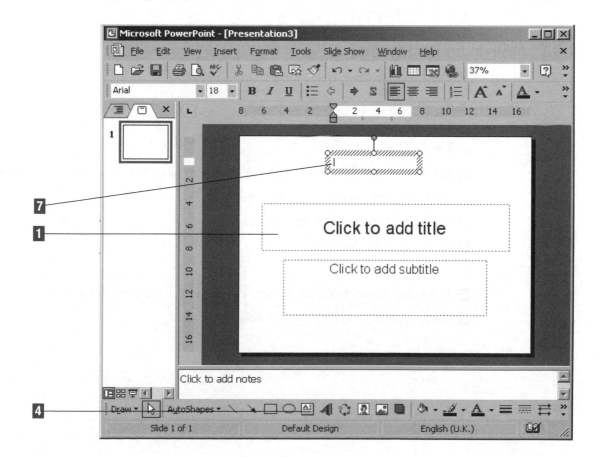

### 1.8.2  Adding Text to the Outline

1. *Click next to the Slide image.*

2. *Start typing.*

3. *You will see the text appear on the slide at the same time.*

**Why doesn't my text show on the Outline?**

When you add text to a slide by creating a text box, it is interpreted as an object and will not appear in the Outline of the presentation.

## 1.9  Backgrounds

**Assessment Objective 1c**

Slides are more interesting when coloured. As well as plain colours you can apply gradients, patterns or add pictures to display in the background. You can even select from a range of slide designs.

### 1.9.1  Applying a Background

1. *Right click a slide.*

Or

2. *Click Format.*

3. *Click Background.*

4. *Click the drop down arrow in the small window to select from a limited range of colours.*

5. *Click Fill Effects for gradients and patterns.*

6. *Click More Colors to open the Colors box.*

7. *Click a colour to select it.*

8. *Click OK.*

9. *In the Background box, click Apply to limit the colour to the current slide.*

10. *Click Apply to All to colour all the slides the same.*

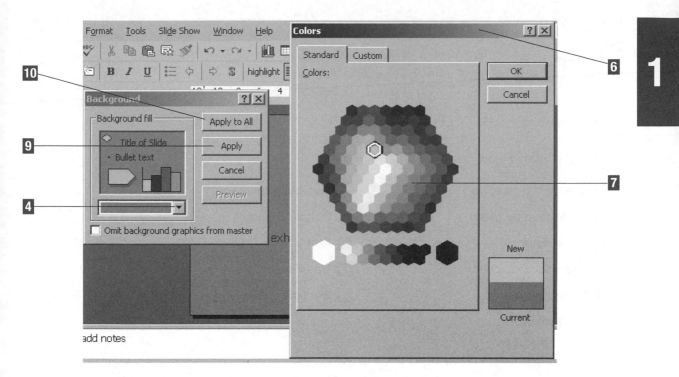

**What colours are best for a presentation?**

Dark backgrounds may not be suitable for a long print run as they use up a great deal of ink. They may also make it harder to read text or labels. Also, strong colours may be less restful on the eye when viewed during a long presentation.

## 1.10 Exiting PowerPoint

1 *Click the top Close button in the window.*

Or

2 *Click the File menu.*

3 *Click Exit.*

# CHAPTER 2

# Text

## What You'll Do

- → Create a new slide
- → Change slide order
- → Insert text
- → Use the spell checker
- → Format text
- → Set font sizes

- → Use bullets
- → Set alignment
- → Edit text
- → Use Find/Replace
- → Set text level

---

## 2.1 New Slides

**Assessment Objective 2a**

Presentations are made up of a number of slides. For New CLAIT you will be asked to create a three-slide presentation and then add a further slide.

### 2.1.1 Slide Layout

Every slide has a particular layout. A new presentation starts with a Title slide offering placeholders for a title and subtitle, and if you add slides they will have a Title and Text layout by default. Apply a different layout by selecting from the range available.

### 2.1.2 Changing Slide Layout

1. Right click a slide.

Or

2. Click Format.

3. Click Slide Layout.

4. Scroll down to see all the layouts offered.

5. Rest the mouse over any layout to read a description.

6. Click a layout to displace the current one.

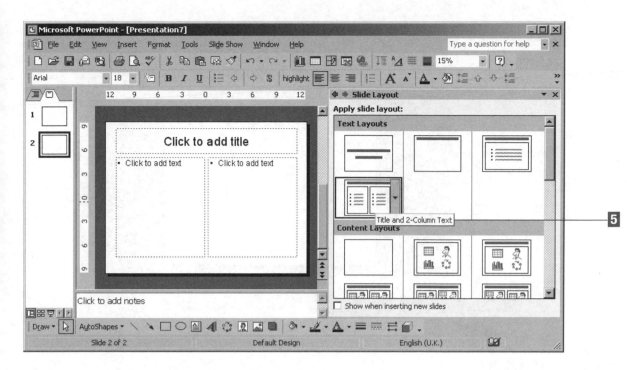

## 2.1.3 Inserting a New Slide

1. *Display the Slides or Outline tab.*

2. *Click a slide thumbnail.*

3. *Press Enter. A new slide will be added below.*

Or

4. *Click the New Slide button in Normal view.*

Or

5. *Click Insert.*

6. *Click New Slide.*

7. *A new slide will appear. It will be the following slide in the presentation.*

8. *To go to a different slide:*

   A. *Click the numbered thumbnail on the Outline or Slides tab.*

   B. *Click the Previous or Next navigation button displaying double arrows to the right of any slide* ⬍.

9. *The number of the slide you are displaying will be shown at the bottom of the window.*

A keyboard shortcut for inserting a new slide is **Ctrl** and **M**.

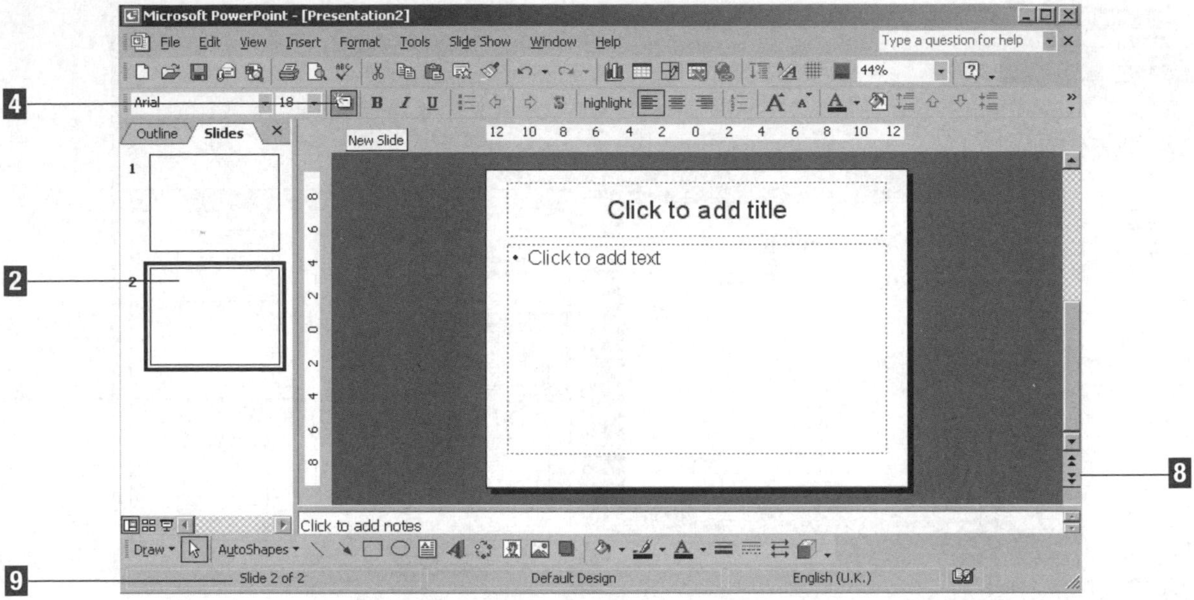

## 2.2 Slide Order

**Assessment Objective 2b**

You can change slide order very quickly if you prefer a particular slide displayed earlier or later in the presentation.

### 2.2.1 Changing Slide Order

**1** *Go to Slide Sorter view.*

Or

**2** *Click the Slides or Outline tab.*

**3** *Click a slide and hold down the mouse button.*

**4** *Drag the slide to a new position when the pointer shows an arrow ending in a box.*

**5** *The position of the slide will be shown by a vertical or horizontal line.*

**6** *Let go of the mouse and the slide will drop into place.*

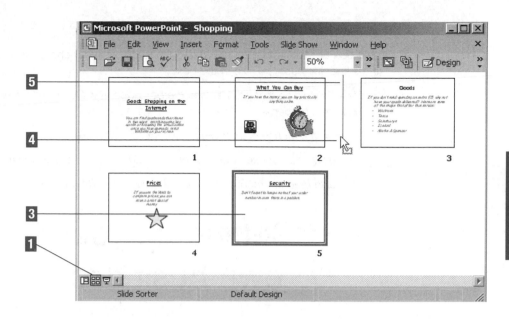

## 2.3 **Inserting Text**

**Assessment Objective 2c**

To add text, you either type it on the Outline tab or type into a placeholder or text box.

When the text appears on the slide, press Enter to move onto the next line. Otherwise, keep typing to fill the box.

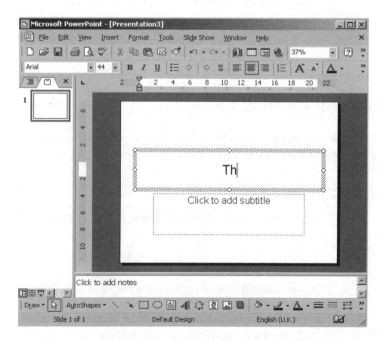

You can increase the size of the box to fit in more text if you want to retain a particular font size.

### 2.3.1 Enlarging a Text Box

If the box or placeholder is not big enough to display your chosen font size or the text on a single line, increase the size of the box:

☐1 *Click the text so that you can see the box edge. It will show white sizing handles and a thickened border.*

☐2 *Position the mouse pointer over a corner sizing handle.*

☐3 *Hold down the mouse button when the pointer shows a two-way arrow.*

☐4 *Click and drag the mouse to draw out the border. The pointer will display a cross.*

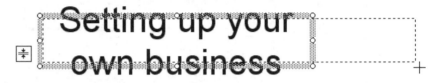

### 2.3.2 Using AutoFit

The AutoFit Options button will appear when you try to fill a placeholder with too much text.

☐1 *Hover over the button to reveal a drop down arrow.*

☐2 *Click the arrow and select an option on the list.*

    ☐A *AutoFit will reduce text size automatically.*

    ☐B *Stop will retain the actual font size.*

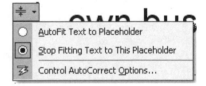

## 2.4 Checking Spelling

Assessment Objective 2d After you have added text to a slide, you need to check it for accuracy. Proof-read on screen and use the spell checker to correct any spelling errors.

### 2.4.1 Using the Spell Checker

☐1 *Right click a red wavy line and select an alternative spelling.*

Or

☐2 *Click the Spelling toolbar button* ✓.

☐3 *In the Spelling box, accept an alternative or change the word manually.*

☐4 *Click Change to update the document.*

☐5 *Click Ignore to retain the current spelling.*

6. Continue checking through the presentation.

7. Click Close to cancel the spell checker.

## 2.5 Formatting Text

Assessment Objective 2h

Each slide will apply a default font style to headings or main text. Change the font and add emphasis such as bold or italic using the toolbar buttons or via the Font box.

1. *Select the text to be formatted.*

2. *Click a toolbar button for bold, italic or underline* **B** *I* <u>U</u> .

3. *Click the drop down arrow in the Font box to select an alternative font.*

Or

4. *Right click the selected text.*

5. *Click Font.*

6. *Select alternatives in the Font and Font style boxes.*

7. *Click OK.*

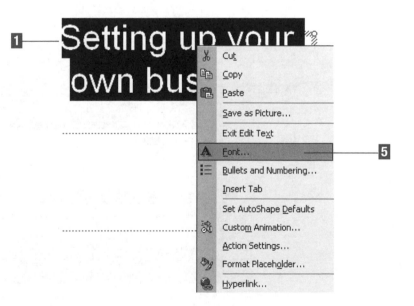

## 2.5.1 Setting Font Size

Assessment
Objective 2e

[1] *Select the text to be formatted.*

[2] *Click the Increase Font Size button to increase the size in stages.*

[3] *Reverse the change by clicking the Decrease Font Size button.*

Or

[4] *Click the drop down arrow in the Font Size box.*

[5] *Click a measure on the list.*

Or

[6] *Type your own measure over any showing in the box.*

[7] *Press Enter to confirm the setting.*

Or

[8] *Click the Format menu.*

[9] *Click Font.*

[10] *Click or type in a measure in the Font Size box.*

[11] *Click OK.*

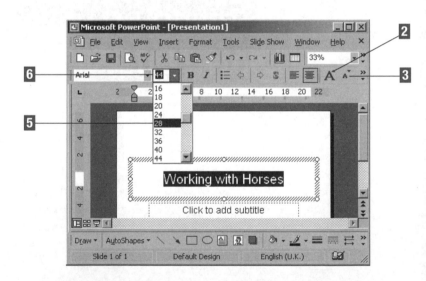

### My text reverts to a different size!

You must confirm a changed text size by pressing Enter. Click the text on the slide and check the figure displayed in the Font Size box to make sure a new size has been applied correctly.

## 2.6 | Using Bullets

**Assessment Objective 2f**
Some text placeholders offer a bulleted list, but you can add bullets to any text and format the bullet style to fit the presentation.

### 2.6.1 Setting Bullets

1. *Select the text to be bulleted.*

2. *Click the Bullets toolbar button.*

Or

3. *Right click and select Bullets and Numbering.*

4. *Click a style of bullet in the window.*

5. *Click OK.*

6. *To remove bullets, select None in the Bullets box.*

Or

7. *Click off the toolbar button.*

8. *If the text in a bulleted list is too close to the bullets, select the text and then drag the marker on the ruler to the right with the mouse.*

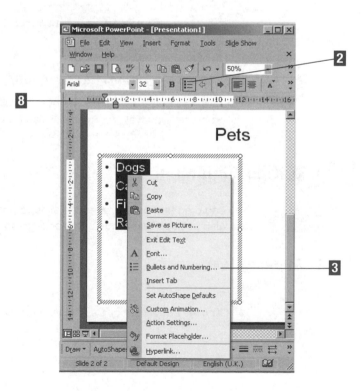

## 2.6.2 Formatting Bullets

1. *Select the bulleted list.*

2. *Right click and select Bullets and Numbering.*

3. *Click the Bulleted tab.*

4. *Click a style of bullet showing in the window.*

5. *Click OK.*

**Why does the text display all different styles of bullet?**

You will find that the default style of bullet differs for each level of text. Select the appropriate text level to format that particular bullet style.

## 2.7 Setting Alignment

**Assessment Objective 2g**

You can drag text boxes round the slide to position them centrally or nearer an edge. You can also position text inside a box or placeholder centrally, or align it right or left.

## 2.7.1 Aligning Text

1. *Select the text.*

2. *Click the Left, Right or Centre Align button on the toolbar.*

## 2.8 Editing and Deleting Text

**Assessment Objective 2i**

Use the same techniques as you would when word processing to delete, copy or move text on a slide or between slides.

- Select the text, click Cut and then Paste to move text to a different position on a slide or to a different slide.

- Select the text, click Copy and then Paste to place a copy of text on a slide.

- Select the text and then press Delete to remove it. In a list, use the Backspace to close up any gaps.

## 2.9 Using Find/Replace

**Assessment Objective 2j**

Replace the same entry throughout a presentation by using the Replace tools provided by PowerPoint.

### 2.9.1 Replacing Text

1. *Click the Edit menu.*

2. *Click Replace.*

3. *Type the word you are looking for into the Find what: box exactly as it appears.*

4. *Type the replacement text into the Replace with: box.*

5. *Click Match case to replace only words where the letters match lower or upper case.*

6. *Click Find whole words only to make sure parts of words will not be replaced.*

7. *Click Replace All if you are sure the criteria are correct.*

8. *Click Find Next to view the next matching word.*

9. *Click Replace to replace the word or Find Next to move on to the next word.*

You can open the Replace box by holding **Ctrl** and pressing **H**.

### My headings have been replaced incorrectly!

Check through the presentation after using the Replace tool to make sure initial capitals are correct in replaced words.

**Text Levels**

PowerPoint recognises levels of text on each slide. The top level is for headings, the next level for subheadings and so on down through the levels. Each level has a default font and bullet style.

To add text on a new line, you may need to change the level by promoting the line upwards or demoting it downwards.

## 2.10.1 Setting Text Levels in Outline View

1. *When starting a presentation, click next to Slide 1 and start typing the heading.*

2. *Press Enter. This will create a new slide.*

3. *To create a heading on Slide 2, keep typing.*

4. *To add text at a lower level on any slide, press Enter.*

5. *Now demote the line:*

   A. *Press the Tab key*

   Or

   B. *Click the Demote arrow on the toolbar.*

6. *Type the lower level text on the slide.*

7. *Press Enter.*

8. *Keep typing and pressing Enter to add new lines at the same level.*

9. *Demote a line to add text at an even lower level.*

10. *You can promote the text to reach a higher level:*

    A. *Hold Shift as you press the Tab key.*

    Or

    B. *Click the Promote arrow.*

11. *To insert a line, click at the end of the line above, press Enter and then set the correct level for the line.*

12. *On the Outline tab, if you keep promoting the line you will eventually reach the top level which creates a new slide.*

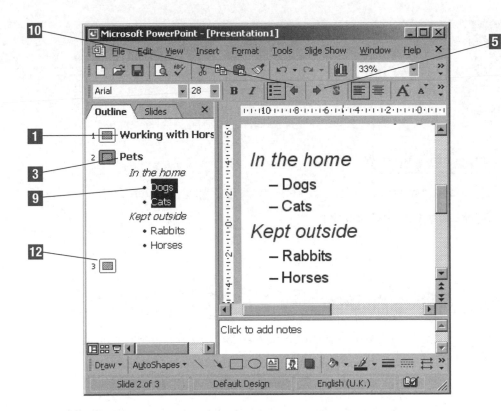

## 2.10.2 Setting Text Levels on a Slide

1. *Click any line.*

2. *Click the Demote arrow to take it down a level.*

3. *Click the Promote arrow to move it up a level.*

# CHAPTER 3

# Images

## What You'll Do

→ Insert a graphic

→ Insert lines and shapes

→ Apply shading

## 3.1 Adding Pictures

**Assessment Objective 3a**

There are three main sources for pictures added to a presentation:

- Those available in the Microsoft Clip Art Gallery.

- Images acquired directly from a camera or scanner.

- Images saved on your computer or removable storage media.

To insert pictures from the Gallery, either use the Clip Art placeholder to open a Select Picture box, or use Insert Clip Art to open the search Task pane.

### 3.1.1 Inserting Clip Art

**1** *Click the Clip Art icon in a placeholder.*

Or

**2** *Click the Insert Clip Art toolbar button on the Drawing toolbar.*

Or

**3** *Click the Insert menu.*

**4** *Click Picture.*

**5** *Click Clip Art.*

**6** *Enter a search word or phrase into the Search text: box.*

**7** *Click the Search button.*

**8** *Scroll through the pictures.*

**9** *Click a picture.*

**10** *Click OK in the Select Picture box to add the picture to the slide and close the box.*

**11** *Click Modify in the Task pane to carry out a new search.*

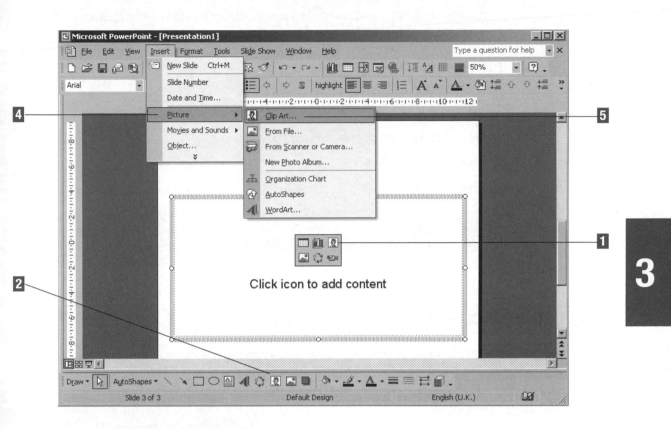

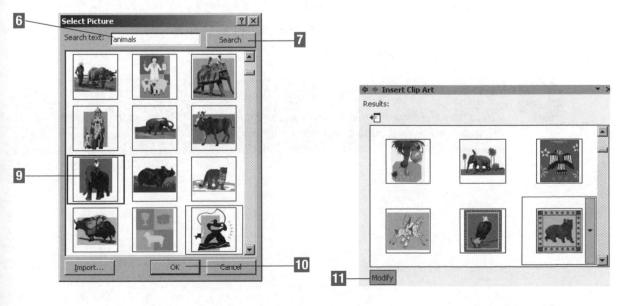

### 3.1.2 Inserting Images from File

For New CLAIT you will be provided with the images you must add to your presentation.

1. *Click the Insert Picture icon*  *in a placeholder or on the Drawing toolbar.*

Or

2. *Click the Insert menu.*

3. *Click Picture.*

4. *Click From File.*

5. *Browse through the pictures on your computer.*

6. *Click the target picture.*

7. *Click Insert or press Enter.*

> **✕ Critical Error**
> Inserting the wrong image or failing to insert the specified image.

## 3.2 Editing Pictures

The picture will appear on the slide in a selected state, showing white circular sizing handles round the edge and a green circle at the end of a rotate arm.

### 3.2.1 Moving a Picture

1. *Position the pointer over the picture.*

2. *Click and hold down the mouse button. You will see a four-headed arrow.*

3. *Drag the picture across the slide.*

> **Warning**
> Take care to follow the instructions. A common mistake is to move the image to the wrong position or to hide or overlap underlying text.

## 3.2.2 Resizing a Picture

1. Click the picture to select it.
2. Position the pointer over a corner sizing handle.
3. Click and hold down the button when the pointer shows a two-headed arrow.
4. Drag out the picture border when the pointer shows a cross.
5. Dotted lines will show the outline of the new size.

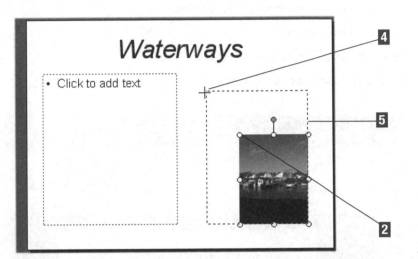

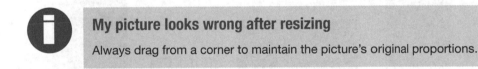

### My picture looks wrong after resizing

Always drag from a corner to maintain the picture's original proportions.

## 3.2.3 Deleting a Picture

1. Click the picture.
2. Press the Delete key.

## 3.3 Lines and Shapes

**Assessment Objective 3b**

Other objects that you can add to a slide include lines, arrows and shapes. These are all available from the Drawing toolbar visible at the bottom of the screen. Once on the slide, resize, move or delete them just as you would a picture.

## 3.3.1 Adding a Drawn Shape

**1** *Click the correct shape or line tool on the toolbar.*

Or

**2** *Click the AutoShapes button to reveal further menus of shapes.*

**3** *Click your preferred shape.*

**4** *Move the mouse over the slide.*

**5** *Click and hold down the mouse button.*

**6** *Drag out the shape.*

**7** *Let go when it is the correct size.*

**8** *You can also click on the slide to add a small shape.*

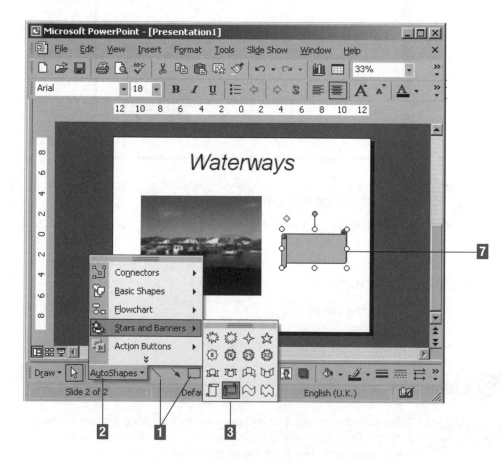

## 3.3.2 Formatting a Shape

The line or shape may already have a coloured border and shapes may be shaded a particular colour. Change the colours or remove them altogether.

1 *Click the shape if it is not selected.*

2 *Click the drop down arrow next to the Line Color button.*

Or

3 *Next to the Fill Color button.*

4 *Select a different colour.*

5 *Click No Line/No Fill to remove the colour.*

Or

6 *Right click the shape.*

7 *Click Format AutoShape.*

8 *Click in the Line or Fill Color boxes.*

9 *Click a different colour.*

10 *Click OK.*

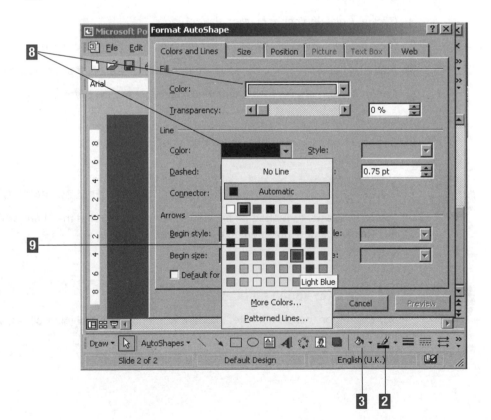

**How do I format text boxes?**

Text boxes and placeholders can be treated like shapes as the borders can be coloured or removed and the box can be filled with colour.

## 3.4 Using the Slide Master

The Slide Master is the slide that controls the background and layout for your slides. (After applying a design, you may need to use a different master for the title slide.) If you want all your slides to be consistent, or to include the same objects such as pictures, shapes or extra text boxes, you don't need to modify every slide individually. Instead you can make a few changes to the Slide Master and these will then be translated throughout the presentation.

### 3.4.1 Working with the Slide Master

1. *Click the View menu.*

2. *Click Master.*

3. *Click Slide Master.*

4. *Click any placeholder to re-align the contents.*

5. *Click different levels of text to format the font, font size, bullet style etc.*

6. *Add a text box or insert pictures or other objects if you want them visible on all slides.*

7. *Return to Normal view by clicking the Close Master View button.*

Or

8. *Click the Normal view button in the corner of the window.*

**Why doesn't changing the Slide Master change the text on my slide?**

If you have already formatted an individual slide, you may find the changes made to the Slide Master are not implemented on that slide.

**Take care with added objects**

If any objects on the Slide Master interfere with entries on individual slides, you must return to the Master view to move or resize them.

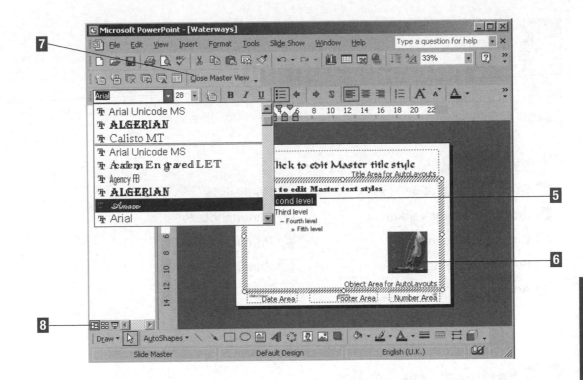

**CHAPTER 4**

# Saving and Printing

## What You'll Do

→ Save a presentation

→ Save a different version

→ Close a presentation

→ Set page orientation

→ Add headers and footers

→ Print slides

→ Print handouts

→ Print an outline

→ Print notes pages

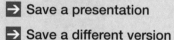 **Saving a Presentation**

| Assessment Objective 4a | PowerPoint files are known as *presentations* and they will contain all the slides in the presentation, as well as any notes pages or handouts. |

### 4.1.1 Saving a Presentation

    ① *Click the Save button.*

Or

    ② *Click the File menu.*

    ③ *Click Save.*

    ④ *Select a location in the Save In: box.*

    ⑤ *Click in the file name box and name the file.*

    ⑥ *Click the Save button or press Enter.*

Click the Save button or hold **Ctrl** and press **S** to update the presentation regularly.

### 4.1.2 Saving a Different Version

| Assessment Objective 4b | To keep separate versions of the presentation: |

    ① *Click the File menu.*

    ② *Click Save As.*

3. Rename the file.

4. Find a new location to save it to if you want to keep it separately.

5. Click the Save button.

## 4.2 Closing a Presentation

**Assessment Objective 4c**

1. Click the lower Close button in the top right hand corner of the window.

Or

2. Click the File menu.

3. Click Close.

## 4.3 Page Orientation

**Assessment Objective 4d**

The default orientation for slides in PowerPoint is landscape, and for handouts, notes or an outline of the presentation it is portrait.

### 4.3.1 Changing Page Orientation

1. Click the File menu.

2. Click Page Setup.

3. Click the correct orientation for slides and/or documents.

4. If necessary, click in the Slides sized for: box to change the size of the item you will eventually print.

5. Click OK.

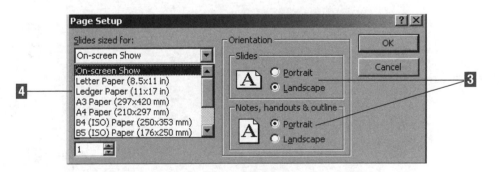

## 4.4 Adding Headers and Footers

**Assessment Objective 4e**

You can add the date, time, slide numbers or text to any slide in the footer area, or add these items to handouts, notes pages or a printed outline.

### 4.4.1 Inserting Headers and Footers

1. Click the Insert menu.

2. Click Date and Time or Slide Number to open the Header and Footer box.

3. Click in the Date and time box.

4. To display the current date whenever the file is opened, click Update automatically.

5. Click in the box to select a style of date or time.

6. For a fixed date, click the radio button.

7. Type in the date using your preferred style.

8. For slide numbers, add a tick to the Slide number box.

9. For a footer, click in the Footer box and type the text in the empty window.

10. Check the preview to see where the items will be placed on the slide. You can drag the boxes to other positions later.

11. Click Apply to add the footer to a single slide.

12. Click Apply to All to add the same items to all slides in the presentation.

13. For documentation, click the Notes and Handouts tab.

14. Repeat the process. You will find you can also add header text.

15. Click OK to leave the box.

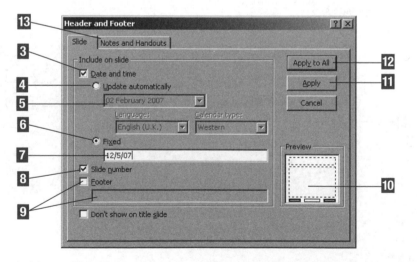

In Master Slide view, there is also a Footer Area box that you can type directly into.

## 4.5 Printing

There are a number of different parts of the presentation that you can print:

- All the slides.

- One or more individual slides.

- Handouts displaying up to nine thumbnail pictures of the slides on a page.

- Notes pages for individual slides.

- An outline of the presentation.

> ⊗ **Critical Error**
> Missing printouts.

## 4.5.1 Printing Slides

**Assessment Objective 4f**

1. *Click the Print button* 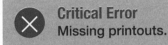 *to print all the slides, one to a page, using the default settings.*

Or

2. *Click the File menu.*

3. *Click Print.*

4. *Click Selection if you have already selected specific slides to print by clicking them when holding down the Shift or Ctrl key.*

5. *Click Current slide to print the slide open on screen.*

6. *Click Slides and then enter a range or individual slide numbers to print only those slides.*

7. *Click in the Copies box to change the number of copies to print.*

8. *To check what will print, click the Preview button.*

9. *Click OK.*

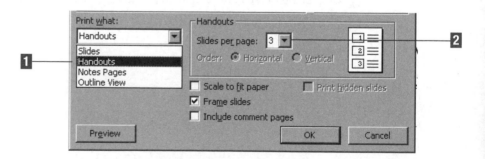

## 4.5.2 Printing Handouts

**1** *In the Print box, click Handouts in the Print what: box.*

**2** *Click the drop down arrow in the Slides per page: box to select a different number of slides to display on each page. You can select 1, 2, 3, 4, 6 or 9 and order them horizontally or vertically.*

### 4.5.3  Printing Notes Pages

1. *To create notes pages, select any slide you will accompany with notes.*

2. *In Normal view, click into the Notes pane to add speaker's notes.*

Or

3. *Click the View menu.*

4. *Click Notes Page.*

5. *Type your notes into the text box below the thumbnail picture of the slide.*

6. *To print Notes Pages, open the Print box.*

7. *If necessary, select individual slides in the Print range: box.*

8. *In the Print what: box click Notes Pages.*

9. *Click OK.*

### 4.5.4  Printing an Outline

**Assessment Objective 4h**

1. *In the Print what: box, click Outline.*

2. *Check that all other settings are correct.*

3. *Click OK.*

**Why does my Outline have slides missing?**

After printing a limited number of slides, future printouts may not include all the slides unless you make sure the print range specifies All. It is a good idea to check in Print Preview before you print out anything.

**4**

### 4.5.5  Printing from Print Preview

1. *Click the Print Preview button* 🔍.

Or

2. *Click the File menu.*

3. *Click Print Preview.*

Or

4. *Click the Preview button in the Print box.*

5. *In the Print what: box, click the drop down arrow and select the item to print.*

6. *Click Options to add a header or footer.*

7. *Click the Print button.*

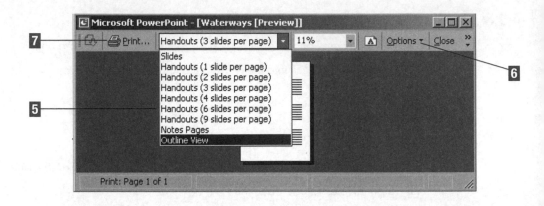

 **Critical Error**
Failing to display all the slides on any printout.

## Learning outcomes

At the end of this unit, you should be able to:

→ Identify and use appropriate software correctly in accordance with laws and guidelines

→ Use basic file handling techniques for the software

→ Download digital pictures from a digital camera

→ Import, crop and resize images

→ Enter, amend and resize text

→ Manipulate and format page items

→ Manage and print artwork

# CHAPTER 1

# Using Images and Shapes

1

## What You'll Do

→ Discover the appropriate software to use

→ Understand image file types

→ Download digital camera images

→ Create artwork

→ Set artwork size and orientation

→ Import images

→ Position images

→ Crop images

→ Resize images

→ Create graphic shapes

## 1.1 The Appropriate Software

**Assessment Objective 1**

This unit has two parts: creating a piece of artwork incorporating pictures, text and shapes, and working with digital camera images.

There is a wide range of programs that can be used when working with digital images: examples include Paint Shop Pro, Photo Shop or Corel Draw. You can create artwork using such programs but the tools are also available within Microsoft Office applications such as Word, PowerPoint or Publisher.

This unit uses Paint Shop Pro and Microsoft Publisher for the examples.

## 1.2 Understanding Graphics

Images can be stored in two different ways: as raster or bitmap graphic images or as vector graphic images.

### 1.2.1 Raster Images

These are made up of grids of coloured dots known as pixels (picture elements), and their quality depends on the image's resolution, which is a measure of the total number of pixels it contains. An image of 640 × 480 pixels, containing 307,200 pixels, for example, will be a lower quality than one of 1280 × 1204 pixels containing over one million pixels.

As it takes a large amount of data to store a high-quality image, data compression techniques are often used to reduce the file size so that images can be stored on disk. But during compression, some detail may be lost.

The main types of bitmap image you will encounter are:

- JPEG (Joint Photographic Experts Group) – used for photos.

- GIF (Graphics Interchange Format) – supports animated images but only 255 colours.

- BITMAP – the file type created when using Microsoft Paint.

Digital cameras normally store photos as JPEGs, but may also offer TIFF (Tagged Image File Format) or RAW (proprietory formats containing minimally processed data) file types.

## 1.2.2 Vector Images

Instead of a collection of pixels, vector images are based on mathematical equations. They can be scaled, rotated or filled without loss of quality. They have a much smaller file size and are mainly used for creating geometric shapes and text.

## 1.3 Digital Camera Images

Having taken some photos with your camera, you need to download them onto the computer before you can edit them. You can then print them out.

## 1.3.1 Downloading Camera Images

**Assessment Objective 1a**

1. Link the camera to your computer's USB port using the cable provided.

Or

2. Take out the memory card and insert that into a card reader plugged into the USB port.

3. Locate the drive containing the images – usually labelled Removable Disk (E: or F:) or a folder inside this.

4. When the images appear, open and save each one or copy them all across into a suitable folder.

5. Rename them as they will have been named generically.

6. If you use software that acquires the photos directly from the camera, you may find they have been moved to a folder within My Pictures labelled with today's date.

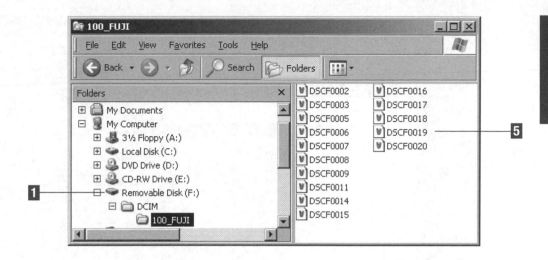

## 1.4 Creating Artwork

You will be asked to create artwork of a specific size and shape and then place pictures, shapes and text within it. The easiest way to do this is to draw the correct size of rectangle or oval on the page and then move the other items inside.

(Opening and working with Publisher files is described in detail in Unit 4.)

### 1.4.1 Setting Artwork Size

**Assessment Objective 1b**

1. *Open Publisher.*

2. *Click New – Blank Publication in the Task pane to open a page on screen.*

3. *Click the shape you want to draw on the Objects toolbar.*

4. *Position the mouse over the page.*

5. *Click and hold down the mouse.*

6. *Drag out the shape.*

7. *Open the Format menu.*

Or

8. *Right click the shape.*

9. *Select Format AutoShape.*

10. *On the Size tab, enter correct width and height measurements into the boxes.*

11. *Click OK to confirm the size.*

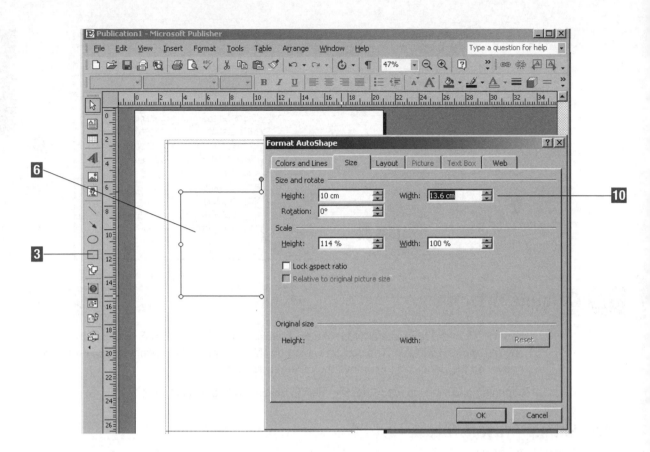

## ℹ What error is allowed?

There is a tolerance of 6 mm both horizontally and vertically on the printed size of the artwork.

## 1.4.2 Artwork Orientation

**Assessment Objective 1b**

You may require a wide rather than tall page for your artwork. Set this by changing to landscape orientation.

☐1 *Click on the File menu.*

☐2 *Click Page Setup.*

▌3 *On the Layout tab, click in the radio button for landscape orientation.*

☐4 *Click OK.*

## 1.5 Importing Images

**Assessment Objective 1c**

There are several ways to add a picture to your page:

- Insert Clip Art from the gallery.

- Insert a picture saved on disk or elsewhere on the computer.

- Acquire an image directly from a camera or scanner.

You could also open the image and then use copy and paste techniques to add it to the page.

For New CLAIT, you will be provided with one or more images that you must insert.

> ⊗ **Critical Error**
> Failing to import the specified image.

### 1.5.1 Inserting a Picture from File

1. *Click the Insert menu.*

2. *Click Picture – From File.*

Or

3. *Click the Picture Frame button on the Objects toolbar.*

4. *Draw a frame into your artwork to take the picture.*

5. *Browse through the drives on your computer to locate the picture to insert.*

6. *Select it in the window.*

7. *Click Insert.*

8. *It will appear on the page.*

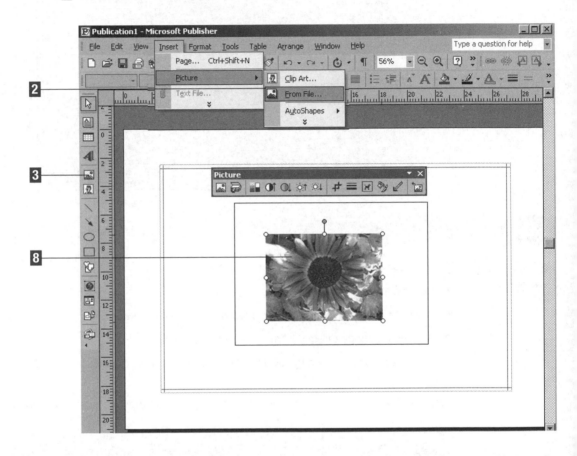

## 1.6 Positioning/Moving Images

**Assessment Objective 1d**

When the picture appears on the page, it must be placed in the correct position in the artwork.

1. *Click the picture to select it.*

2. *Position the pointer over the picture.*

3. *When it shows a van displaying the word 'Move', hold down the mouse button.*

4. *Drag the picture into the artwork when the pointer shows a four-headed arrow.*

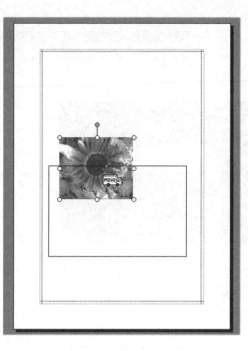

**Warning**

Make sure that the image does not touch or overlap any other items.

## 1.7   Cropping Images

Assessment
Objective 1e

Unwanted parts of a picture round the edges can be removed by cropping.

1. *Right click the picture and select Show Picture Toolbar.*

2. *Click the Crop tool.*

3. *Black lines will appear round the picture.*

4. *Move the mouse to one of the black lines on the border. The pointer will show a T or corner shape.*

5. *Click and hold down the mouse button.*

6. *Drag the selected border inwards. A dotted line will show its new position.*

7. *Let go of the mouse and the part of the picture outside the dotted line will disappear.*

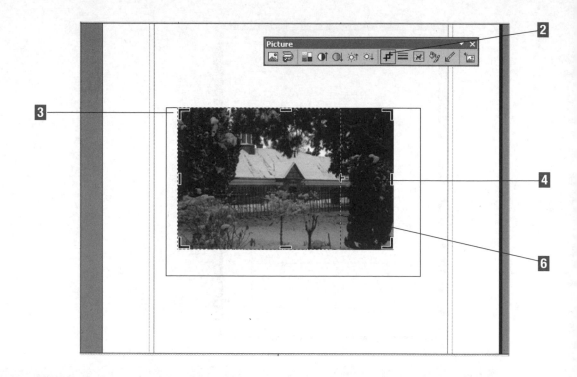

## 1.8 Resizing Images

**Assessment Objective 1f**

If you don't draw a frame to take the picture, it can be very large when it first appears. Resize it so that it is easier to work with, as well as letting you fit it into the artwork.

### 1.8.1 Changing Picture Size

1. *If you cannot see any edges when it appears, drag the picture across the page until you see one.*

2. *Position the mouse over a corner white sizing handle.*

3. *When it shows an arrow labelled 'Resize', click and hold down the mouse button.*

4. *Gently drag the border in or out. The pointer will show a cross.*

Or

5. *Right click and select Format Picture.*

6. *Change the width or height measurements on the Size tab.*

7. *Click Lock aspect ratio to keep the picture in proportion.*

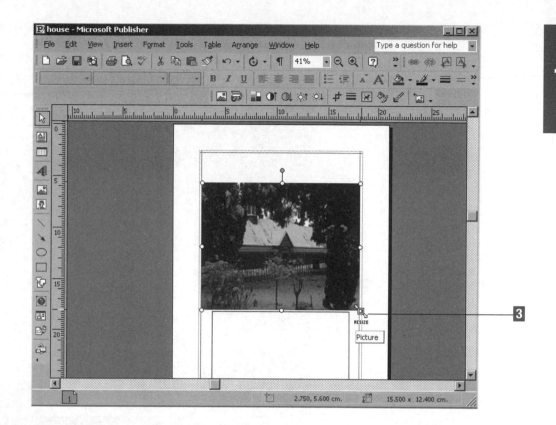

## 1.9 Creating Graphic Shapes

**Assessment Objective 1g**

There are a number of ready-made shapes that are available in all Microsoft Office programs. These range from rectangles, ovals and lines to complex shapes such as stars and banners or those used in flow charts.

After a shape is created, it can be resized, coloured, rotated or copied.

### 1.9.1 Drawing Shapes

**1** *Click the shape toolbar button or select a shape from the AutoShape menu.*

**2** *Move the pointer over the page.*

**3** *Click to place the shape on the page. The rectangle will produce a square and the oval will produce a circle.*

**4** *Click and hold down the mouse button as you draw out the shape to control the size.*

**5** *For some types of line, you may need to double click the mouse to release the pointer.*

**6** *Hold down **Ctrl** when using the mouse if you want to draw out a square or circle.*

Here's a tip – keep a line straight by holding **Shift** as you draw it out. Draw a line centred on your starting point by holding **Ctrl** as you draw.

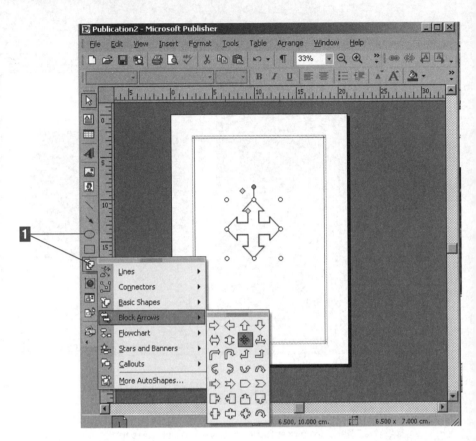

# Adding and Amending Text

## What You'll Do

→ Insert text
→ Resize text to fit

→ Amend text

2

## 2.1  Inserting Text

**Assessment
Objective 2a**

You can add text to a page in Publisher by typing it into a text box. You can also add text to a photograph using an image editing program.

### 2.1.1  Inserting Text in Publisher

Draw a text box on the page first and then enter the text. You can rotate the text by dragging round the text box and show the background colours behind it by making it transparent or removing any fill colour.

**1** *Click the Text Box tool.*

**2** *Draw a text box on the page.*

**3** *Start typing where the cursor is flashing.*

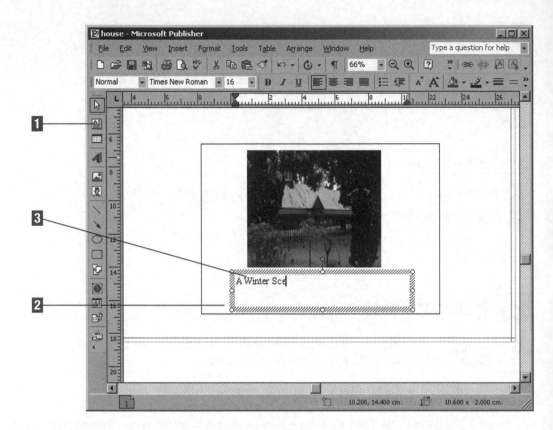

<table>
<tr><td>⊗</td><td>Critical Error<br>Failing to enter the correct text.</td></tr>
</table>

## 2.1.2 Adding Text in Paint Shop Pro

Once you open a photo in a program such as Paint Shop Pro, you can add text using the Text tool.

**1** *Click the Text tool.*

**2** *Click on the photo.*

**3** *In the Text Entry box that will open, enter your text.*

**4** *Select an appropriate font and font size.*

**5** *Keep it as a Vector graphic so that it can be rescaled and edited.*

**6** *Click OK to add it to the photo.*

**7** *It will show deformation handles round the edge so you can drag one of these to resize the text if it is too small to be visible clearly.*

**8** *Text is added on its own layer. Once you have started editing another part of the photo, you must activate the correct layer before you can make changes to the text.*

**9** *Click the Layer Palette button.*

**10** *Click the Text layer in the palette to activate it.*

**11** *Click the Object Selector toolbar button.*

**12** *Click the text object you want to amend.*

**13** *Move or resize it on screen or right click, select Edit Text and return to the Text Entry box.*

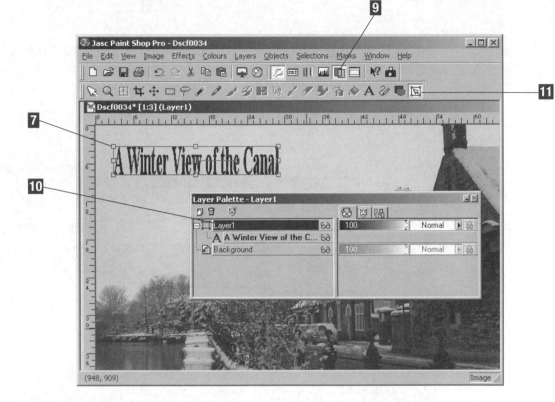

## 2.1.3  Resizing Text in Publisher

To fill a text box, you can increase the font size of any text and also add extra spacing between characters. Changing spacing is known in typography as kerning.

1️⃣ *Select the text.*

2️⃣ *Click the Increase Font Size button repeatedly to increase the font size in steps.*

3️⃣ *Select an exact measure in the font size box if you know the size of text you want.*

4️⃣ *Click the Format menu.*

5️⃣ *Click Character Spacing.*

6️⃣ *Change the tracking or kerning settings if a small amount of extra space is needed between characters.*

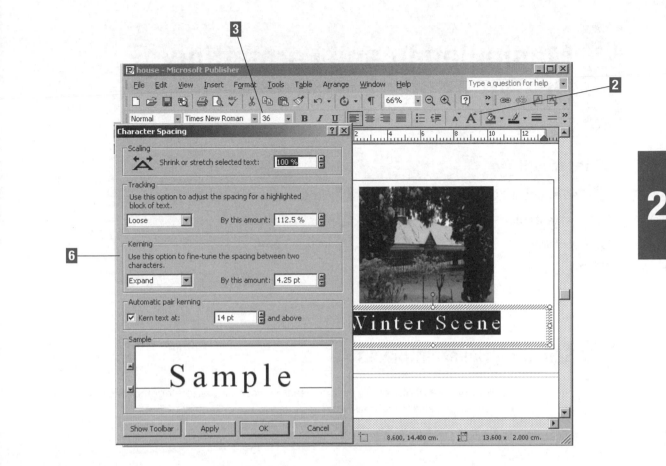

## 2.2 Amending Text

**Assessment Objective 2b**

You will be asked to change the text you have entered into your artwork.

1. Click into the text, type extra characters and use the Delete and Backspace keys to make any changes.

2. Take care not to introduce any spelling mistakes.

3. Click an alignment button to set the text to the left, right or in the centre of the text box

.

# CHAPTER 3

# Manipulating and Formatting Drawn Items

## What You'll Do

➔ Use specified colours

➔ Rotate items

➔ Flip items

➔ Copy items

➔ Crop items

➔ Resize items

➔ Delete items

## 3.1 Selecting Several Objects

If you want several objects to have the same colour, be resized together or be removed at the same time, select them all first:

1. *Click the first, hold down **Ctrl** and click subsequent objects.*

Or

2. *Click the Select Objects*  *tool on the Objects toolbar.*

3. *Click and hold down the mouse button and then draw a box round the items you want to select.*

4. *Let go and they will all remain selected.*

## 3.2 Using Specified Colours

**Assessment Objective 3a**

Shapes can be filled with colour and borders can be coloured, restyled or removed altogether. Use either the toolbar buttons or the Format menu options to make changes.

### 3.2.1 Filling Shapes

1. *Click the shape.*

2. *Click the Fill Color button to add the colour showing under the paint pot.*

3. *Click the drop down arrow next to the button to select from a wider range of colours.*

4 *Click a box to add that colour, or click More Colors.*

5 *When the palette opens, click a colour.*

6 *Drag the transparency slider across or set a different percentage in the box to increase transparency.*

7 *Click No Fill to remove any colour.*

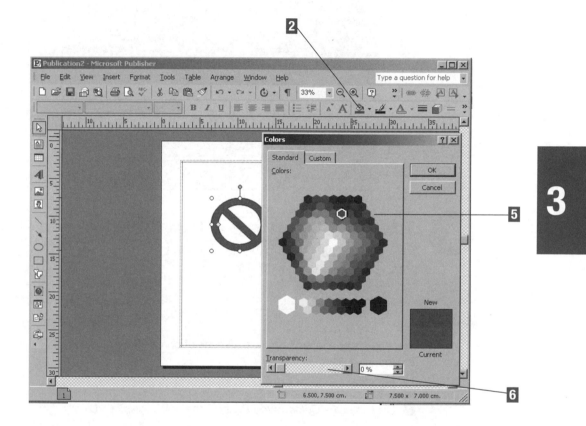

Or

8 *Click the Format menu or right click the shape.*

9 *Click Format AutoShape.*

10 *On the Colors and Lines tab, click the drop down arrow in the Color box to select a different fill colour.*

11 *Click OK to confirm the new settings.*

**What do I do if my text box is white but the slide has a coloured background?**

To reveal the background colour of the artwork under any text, choose No Fill or change the text box transparency to 100 per cent.

## 3.2.2 Borders

You can set a different style or thickness of border, including dotted or double lines, as well as apply a colour.

1. *Click the shape or text box.*

2. *Click the Line Color button to apply the colour displayed.*

3. *Click the drop down arrow to find a different colour.*

4. *Click the Line/Border Style button to find a different style of line.*

5. *Click No Line to remove a visible border.*

6. *Click More Lines to open the formatting box.*

7. *Click in the Line Color box to change the colour.*

8. *Click to set a different style of dashed line.*

9. *Click to set a different style of solid line.*

10. *Click to increase or decrease the line weight.*

11. *Click OK to confirm the new settings.*

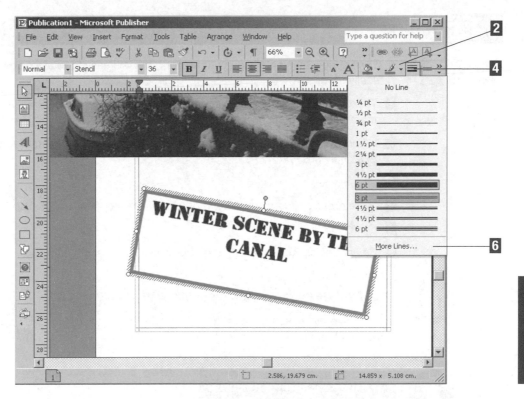

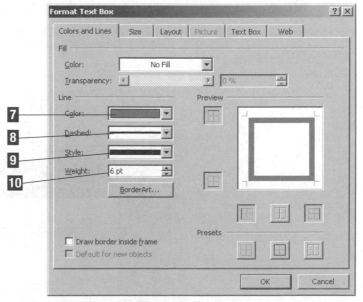

**Warning**

Take care to remove the text box border round your text if instructed to do so.

## 3.3 Rotating

Text will appear horizontally on your artwork, but it is easy to rotate it so that it reads vertically up or down.

**1** *To rotate a text box or any shape by hand, position the pointer over the green circle at the end of the rotate arm.*

**2** *When you see circular arrows, hold down the mouse button and drag the object round to its new position.*

Or

**3** *Set a rotate option by clicking to open the Arrange menu.*

**4** *Click Rotate or Flip.*

**5** *Select Left or Right to rotate the object by 90° in that direction.*

### I get confused between clockwise and anticlockwise

Clockwise will make text read down from the top, anticlockwise will make text read up from the bottom.

### My shape has flipped right over!

If you drag too vigorously you can flip the shape vertically by mistake. To put things right, either drag it back again or use the Undo option.

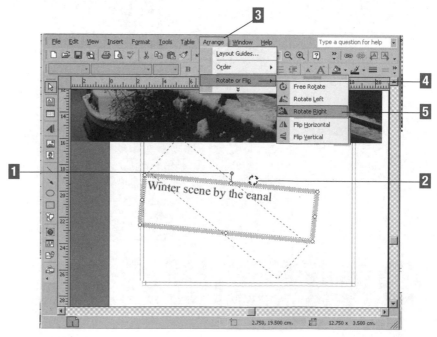

**Is there any difference between the two rotation methods?**

You should use a rotate option rather than rotate by dragging if you want to rotate objects accurately.

## 3.4  Flipping

Assessment
Objective 3c

Change your picture so that it faces the other way, vertically or horizontally, by applying a flip option. A horizontal flip becomes a mirror image.

### 3.4.1  Flipping a Shape

1. *Click the shape.*
2. *Click to open the Arrange menu.*
3. *Click Rotate or Flip.*
4. *Click Flip Horizontal or Vertical.*

**3**

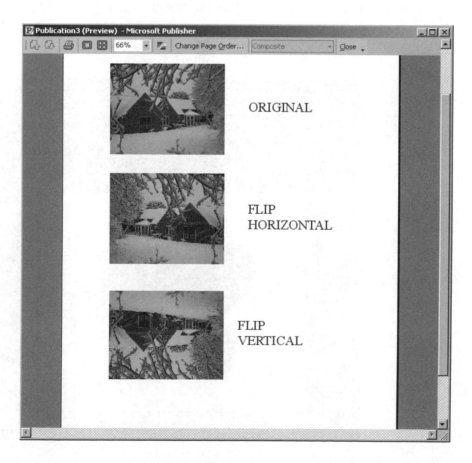

## 3.5 Copying

**Assessment Objective 3d** Once you have created a shape and perhaps applied some colour, make exact replicas quickly using the copy function.

### 3.5.1 Copying a Shape

1. *Click the shape.*

2. *Select Copy. Right click, click the toolbar button or select this option on the Edit menu.*

3. *Click on the page to take off the selection on the original shape.*

4. *Click Paste.*

5. *Keep clicking Paste to add more copies to the page.*

6. *Drag individual shapes into position on the artwork.*

Or

7. *Hold down **Ctrl** as you drag a shape to a new position to create a copy.*

You can also use the keyboard shortcuts: **Ctrl–C** to copy and **Ctrl–V** to paste.

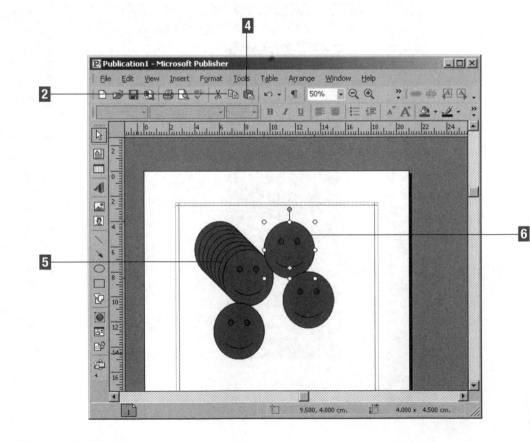

## 3.6 Cropping

**Assessment Objective 3e**

See Section 1.7 Cropping Images on page **231**.

## 3.7 Resizing

**Assessment Objective 3f**

Change the size of any shape by dragging the border in or out or set an exact size.

1. *Click the shape.*

2. *Position the pointer over a corner sizing handle, to maintain the proportions.*

3. *Click and hold down the mouse button.*

4. *Drag the border in or out.*

Or

5. *Right click and select Format AutoShape.*

6. *On the Size tab, enter an exact width or height measurement.*

7. *Click Lock aspect ratio to maintain proportions.*

8. *Many shapes display a yellow triangle – click and drag this to exaggerate one aspect.*

**3**

## 3.8 Deleting

**Assessment Objective 3g**

Remove an unwanted object in the following way:

1. *Select it and press the Delete key.*

2. *Right click and select Delete on the menu.*

# CHAPTER 4

# Managing and Printing Artwork

## What You'll Do

→ Create artwork

→ Understand resolution

→ Set resolution

→ Save artwork

→ Save digital images

→ Print artwork

→ Close artwork

## 4.1 Creating Artwork

**Assessment Objective 4a**

There are different ways that artwork and photographs can be displayed, for example:

- On paper.

- On a computer monitor.

- On a web page.

- On a television screen.

- On a digital camera Liquid Crystal Display screen.

When printing your artwork, you can produce a full colour image or you can print in black and white (or greyscale). When using a DTP program, you can show all the colours on one page (a composite copy) or print a single page for each colour (printing separations) to show how they are laid out.

## 4.2 Understanding Resolution

The quality of your photo depends on its resolution – described on page **225**. When printing onto paper, this needs to be much higher (200–300 dots per inch or dpi) than when displayed on a computer monitor. Here a resolution of 72 pixels per inch (ppi) is quite adequate.

The number of pixels in an image remains the same so that, when you increase resolution, the picture size will decrease and vice versa. Re-set width and height measurements if you want to print the picture at its original size.

### 4.2.1 Changing Resolution in Paint Shop Pro

Assessment
Objective 4b

[1] *Open the photo.*

[2] *Click to open the Image menu.*

[3] *Click Resize.*

[4] *Change the measurement in the Resolution box.*

[5] *Check if you want pixels per inch or per cm.*

[6] *Click in the width or height box and edit the measurement so the actual picture size is roughly the same as the original.*

[7] *Click OK.*

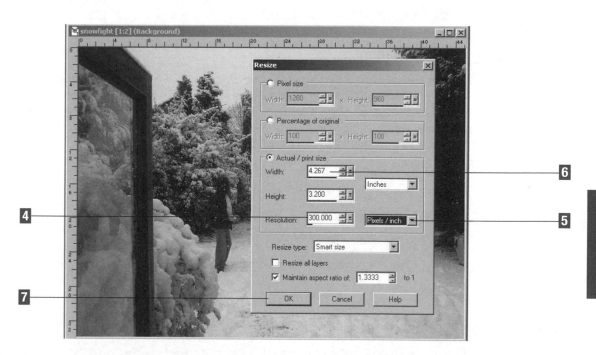

## 4.3 Saving and Closing Artwork

Assessment
Objective 4c

When using Publisher, you save the artwork exactly as you save a publication.

### 4.3.1 Saving Artwork for the First Time

[1] *Click the Save button.*

Or

[2] *Open the File menu.*

3. Click Save.

4. Select a suitable location for the file.

5. Click in the File name: box and type a name for your artwork.

6. Click Save.

## 4.3.2 Saving a Different Version

1. Click to open the File menu.

2. Click Save As.

3. Type a new name for the artwork and/or select a different save location.

4. Click Save.

## 4.3.3 Saving Digital Images

Images are saved on a camera with generic names such as DSCF0001, DSCF0002 etc. Once downloaded, save them with sensible names into a folder such as My Pictures or one you have created specially. If opened into Paint Shop Pro or another image editing program, decide if you want to save your photos in JPEG format or as a program-specific file (such as .PSP) where the layers will be maintained.

1. Click to open the File menu.

2. Click Save As.

3. Select a folder location.

4. Rename the picture file.

5. Check that the correct file format is selected in the Save as type: box.

6. Click Save.

## 4.3.4 Closing Artwork

Close your artwork in the same way that you close any Publisher file.

1. Click to open the File menu.

2. Click Close.

Or

3. Click the Close button on the title bar.

## 4.4 Printing Artwork

**Assessment Objective 4d**

This unit is the only one where you must print in colour. You must also print a photograph in black and white.

1. *Click to open the File menu.*

2. *Click Print.*

3. *Click Properties (or the appropriate button, depending on your printer).*

4. *Click the tab where the colour is set.*

5. *Click to select colour or black and white/greyscale.*

6. *Click OK.*

**4**

**3**

**4**

**Print**
Printer
Name: Brother MFC-5440CN Printer   Properties...
Status: Ready

**Brother MFC-5440CN Printer Properties**

Basic | Advanced | Support

Photo

Colour/Greyscale    ● Colour
                    ○ Greyscale

**5**

Image Type          ○ Auto
                    ● Photo
                    ○ Graphics
                    ○ Custom          Setting

MFC will stop Colour/Greyscale print operations when one or more
of the ink cartridges are empty.                    Default

OK    Cancel    Help

---

✖ **Critical Error**
Failing to print artwork displaying the correct colours.

✖ **Critical Error**
Failing to print any suitable digital image.

✖ **Critical Error**
Missing printouts.

## 4.5 Exiting the Application

When you click the Close button at the top of a publication you also exit Publisher.
Otherwise, exit the application from the menu:

1 *Click to open the File menu.*

2 *Click Exit.*

## Learning outcomes

At the end of this unit, you should be able to:

→ Identify and use appropriate software correctly

→ Import, format and place text and image files

→ Insert relative, external and email hyperlinks

→ Manage and print web pages

# CHAPTER 1

# Working with FrontPage

## What You'll Do

→ Know the parts of a web page

→ Discover web authoring software

→ Launch FrontPage

→ Create a document

→ Save a web page

→ Open an existing web page

→ Close a web page

→ Exit the application

## 1.1  Web Pages

The multimedia documents that make up the World Wide Web are known as web pages. You can view them only by using an application known as a browser. Examples include Internet Explorer, Netscape, Mozilla's Firefox and Opera.

When a website is created, it can consist of hundreds of web pages, images, coloured backgrounds, video clips, sound files etc. which relate to each other and so must all be published over the Internet together. To keep all the files together and the web page links working correctly, you should store them in the same folder.

### 1.1.1  Web Page Structure

Here are the main aspects of a web page:

**1** *A single web page will fill the main window of your browser and display coloured text, images and other objects.*

**2** *Many parts of a web page have built-in links – hyperlinks. If clicked when the pointer shows a hand, they open a new page or email application.*

**3** *Buttons on the browser toolbar allow you to work with the page and access different web pages.*

**4** *A web page is written in special code, HTML (HyperText Markup Language), so that it can be interpreted by all browsers.*

**5** *You can print the HTML code as well as the whole page, or print images from the page separately. (See Chapter 8 for more information about web pages.)*

6 *Each web page has a title that is displayed in the title bar of the browser and a unique address that shows where the page is stored.*

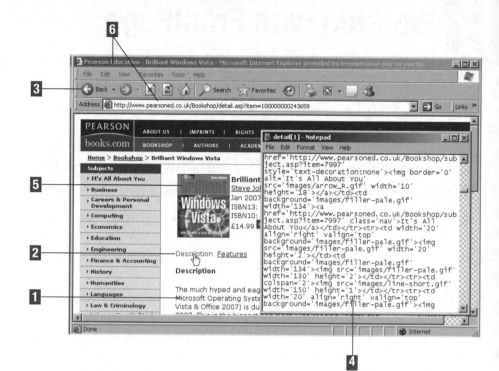

Source: Pearson Education Limited

## 1.2 Web Authoring Software

Although it is handy to know how to write HTML code, applications are now available to do that for you. You create a page as if you were word processing a document and the underlying code will be written at the same time. Some of the software simply helps design pages, but other applications provide guidance on setting up and running complex websites.

This chapter uses Microsoft FrontPage for the examples, but other applications available include Dreamweaver, Namo WebEditor, Magix Website Maker, Web Design Studio, Vcom Web Easy Professional and EasyGen.

If you use modern word processing, DTP or some other applications, you will be able to view and publish your documents as web pages. However, dedicated web authoring software offers far more facilities and so should be used for serious web page creation.

## 1.3 Launching FrontPage

    1. *Click the Start button.*

    2. *Click All Programs.*

    3. *Click Microsoft FrontPage.*

Or, if you have a shortcut to the program on the desktop, click the icon

    Microsoft FrontPage .

## 1.4 The Opening Screen

When FrontPage opens, you will see a new blank web page and standard and formatting toolbars. On the left are links to different views, but you will not need to view the page in any other than Page view for New CLAIT.

There are three different view modes for working on a web page:

    **1** *Normal* – this is where you add text and images and build up the page.

    **2** *HTML* – click this to view the underlying code.

    **3** *Preview* – see how the page will look in a browser.

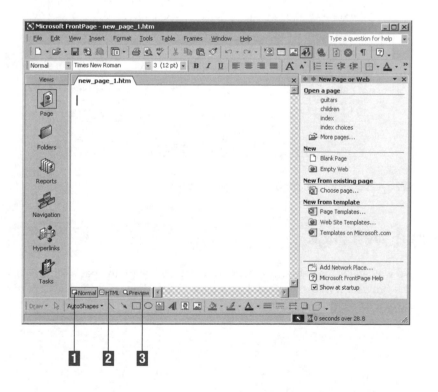

## 1.5 Creating a New Page

Assessment
Objective 1a

When you create new pages in FrontPage, all the open pages are visible as named tabs at the top of the screen. Move between open pages by clicking their tab.

1 *Click Blank Page in the New Page or Web Task pane.*

Or

2 *Click the File menu.*

3 *Click New. This opens the Task pane.*

Or

4 *Click the New toolbar button.*

5 *The new page will add a new tab at the top of the page labelled new_page_2.*

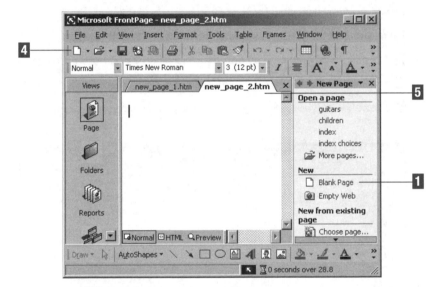

A keyboard shortcut for a new page is **Ctrl–N**.

## 1.6 Saving a Web Page

Assessment
Objective 1c

As well as the file name, you need to choose a title for the page that will show at the top of the browser window. To keep the original intact when you make any changes to the page, save it as a different version.

## 1.6.1 Saving and Naming a Web Page

**1** *Click the Save button.*

Or

**2** *Click the File menu.*

**3** *Click Save.*

**4** *Select a location for the file so that it shows in the Save In: box.*

**5** *Enter a name for the page. The default may appear as* index *as that is the standard name for the opening page of any website.*

**6** *Click the Change title button to edit the page title.*

**7** *Click the Save button or press Enter.*

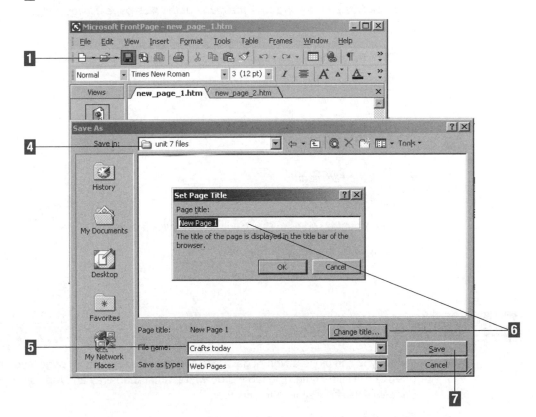

A keyboard shortcut for Save is **Ctrl–S**.

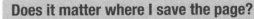

### Does it matter where I save the page?

Make sure you select the correct folder in which to save web pages, and that you name them correctly. Their file and folder location will be displayed when you print.

### 1.6.2　Saving a Different Version of the Page

1. *Open the Save As window.*

2. *Change the name in the File name: box and/or change the location in the Save in: box.*

3. *Click Save or press the Enter key.*

## 1.7　Opening an Existing Web Page

There are three choices when opening web pages: find recent pages listed on the File menu; choose from pages listed in the Task pane; or browse through all your computer files.

1. *Click the File menu.*

2. *Click Recent Files and click the name of the web page if listed.*

Or

3. *Click the named page in the New Page Task pane.*

4. *To browse for the file, click More pages in the Task pane.*

Or

5. *Click the Open toolbar button.*

Or

6. *Click the File menu.*

7. *Click Open.*

8. *When the file shows in the main window, click its name.*

9. *Click Open or press the Enter key.*

A shortcut to the Open box is **Ctrl–O**.

## 1.8　Closing a Web Page

Before you can close a web page, make sure it is the uppermost page if you have several open at the same time. The tab will be white rather than grey and the name of the active page will also be visible in the title bar.

1. *Click the page Close button.*

Or

2. *Click the File menu.*

3. *Click Close.*

Or use the keyboard shortcut **Ctrl–W**.

## 1.9 Exiting FrontPage

1. *Click the top Close button.*

Or

2. *Click the File menu.*

3. *Click Exit.*

# CHAPTER 2

# Creating a Web Page

## What You'll Do

→ Enter text

→ Insert a text file

→ Check for errors

→ Insert an image

→ Change alignment

→ Edit a web page

→ Add backgrounds

→ Control text flow

## 2.1 Adding Text

### 2.1.1 Entering and Editing Text

**Assessment Objective 2a**

1. *Start typing where the cursor is flashing.*

2. *Type just as you would when word processing.*

3. *Press Enter to move down two lines.*

4. *To type text on the following line, hold Shift as you press Enter.*

5. *Click into a paragraph and type to insert extra characters.*

6. *Use the Backspace and Delete keys to erase text.*

7. *Drag selected text to a new position on the page.*

8. *Hold down* **Ctrl** *when you drag to copy text to a new position.*

9. *Use cut/copy and paste to move or copy text as described in Chapter 1 (page* **61***).*

**Critical Error**

Failing to include any or all of the specified text.

**Does overtyping work in FrontPage?**

Pressing the Insert key will *not* move you into overtyping mode as it does in Word, so you cannot use this facility to replace text.

## 2.1.2 Inserting a Text File

Assessment Objective 2b

You may want to create web pages that contain text created and saved elsewhere. Do this by inserting a text file straight into the page.

1 *Click the Insert menu.*

2 *Click File.*

3 *In the Select File box, browse for the file on your computer.*

4 *Make sure you change the Files of type: entry to All Files or you will be able to see only HTML files.*

5 *Click the name of the file.*

6 *Click Open.*

7 *The text will appear on the page.*

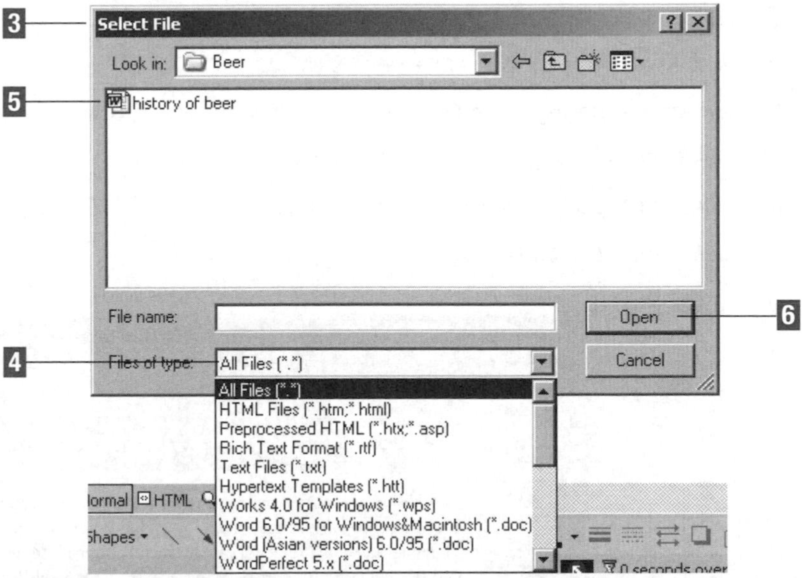
3
5
4
6
Select File
Look in:
Beer
history of beer
File name:
Files of type:
All Files (*.*)
Open
Cancel
All Files (*.*)
HTML Files (*.htm;*.html)
Preprocessed HTML (*.htx;*.asp)
Rich Text Format (*.rtf)
Text Files (*.txt)
Hypertext Templates (*.htt)
Works 4.0 for Windows (*.wps)
Word 6.0/95 for Windows&Macintosh (*.doc)
Word (Asian versions) 6.0/95 (*.doc)
WordPerfect 5.x (*.doc)

**Critical Error**

Not inserting the correct file or making changes to the text that are not asked for.

**Assessment Objective 2c**

Once you have typed a page, check carefully for any errors as the page may be read by thousands of people surfing the web. Mistakes do not give a good impression. When you are designing your own pages, you should also think carefully about how attractive they are to view and how they will be read.

For New CLAIT, be careful not to make any change to an inserted file that is not specifically asked for.

## 2.2.1 Using the Spell Checker

1 *Right click any word showing a red underline and select an alternative if listed.*

2 *Follow the same procedure for grammar errors shown by a green underline.*

3 *Click the Spelling button to work through the page.*

4 *Click Ignore/Ignore All to leave a spelling unchanged.*

5 *Click an alternative if a suitable word is listed.*

6 *Correct the spelling in the Change To: box if no word is suggested.*

7 *Click Change/Change All to update the page.*

8 *Click Add to add the word to the dictionary.*

9 *Click Cancel to close the box.*

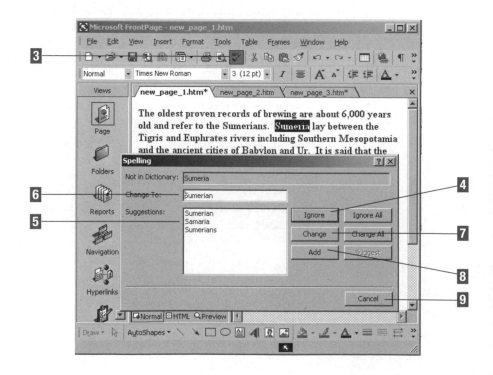

## 2.2.2 Page Content

As you publish web pages on the World Wide Web, it is important that they load quickly. As well as the content being short enough for reading on a monitor, you should try to keep paragraphs brief and use bullet points and subheadings to break up the text. Otherwise readers will become impatient and will stop the page downloading.

Check the figures in the bottom right hand corner of each page to see how long it will take to load. You can then cut some of the content if it is too wordy.

# 2.3 Inserting Images

**Assessment Objective 2d** Many web pages have images included: these break up the text and make the pages more attractive to view. They can be used instead of text as hyperlinks to open different pages.

Although you can add Clip Art images to web pages, they may not be in the right format for the World Wide Web. For New CLAIT, you will be provided with a suitable image to add to your page.

## 2.3.1 Image File Types

Image files suitable for the World Wide Web need to have a small file size so that they download more quickly. The file types that are used for the Web are:

- JPEG/JPG – Joint Photographic Experts Group. This is ideally suited for compressing photographic images. However, it loses quality so that the more you compress the image to try to save file size, the lower the quality of the image will be.
- GIF – Graphics Interchange Format. This compresses the image by reducing the number of colours. GIF images work better for large blocks of colour and sharp edges.
- PNG – Portable Network Graphics. This was designed as a replacement for GIF and is the newest image file format on the Web. It is used to save photographic images and to select certain colours as transparent. When the image is compressed the file size is considerably larger than both JPEG and GIF files.

## 2.3.2 Inserting an Image

1. *Click the Insert menu.*

2. *Click Picture.*

3. *Click From File.*

4. *Browse for the file on your computer.*

5. *Click its name in the window.*

6. *Click Insert.*

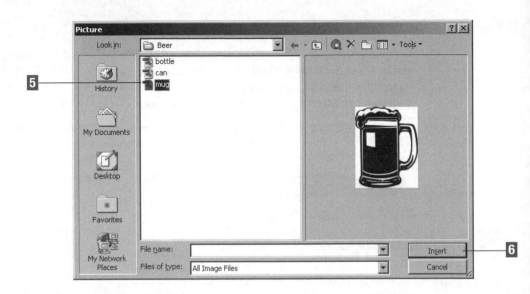

![Picture dialog box]

> **Critical Error**
> Failing to insert the correct image or producing a printout with the image missing.

## 2.4 Formatting Images

When the picture appears, it will display black squares (sizing handles) round the edge. You will not be able to drag it round the page freely, but can move it up or down or position it using the alignment tools.

### 2.4.1 Image Alignment

**Assessment Objective 2e**

1. Click the image if it is not selected.

2. Move the mouse pointer over the image.

3. When the pointer shows a white arrow, click and hold down the pointer.

4. Drag the picture above, below or into the text. This will move out of the way. A vertical line will show the new position for the picture.

5. Let go of the mouse button when the line is positioned correctly and the picture will drop into place.

6. Click an alignment button on the toolbar to place the image on the left, centre or right of the page.

7. For more exact placing, right click the picture and click Picture Properties.

8. On the Appearance tab, click in the Alignment box and select an exact option.

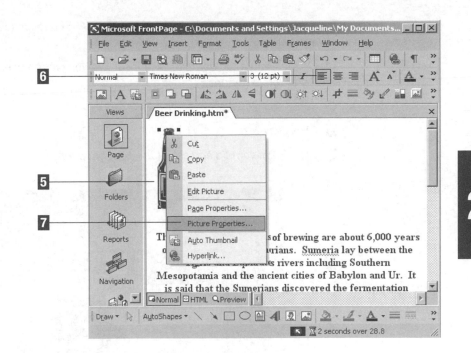

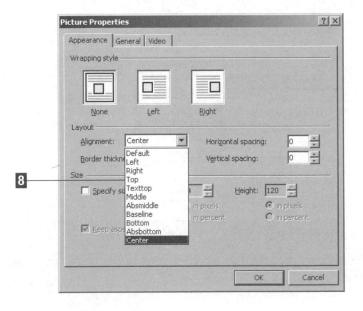

## 2.4.2 Image Size and Orientation

**1** *Click and drag a sizing handle to increase or decrease the size of an image.*

Or

**2** *Right click the picture to open the Picture Properties box.*

3 *On the Appearance tab, click the Size checkbox and set exact measurements for width and height.*

4 *On the Picture toolbar that will appear, change picture orientation by clicking one of the flip or rotate buttons.*

Or

5 *Click Draw.*

6 *Click Rotate or Flip and select the correct option.*

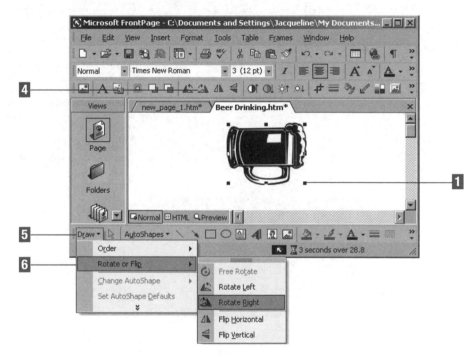

Rotate

### Why does my picture look squashed?

When resizing, always drag from a corner sizing handle so that you keep the image in proportion.

## 2.5 Editing Web Page Elements

Assessment
Objective 2f

When you start using FrontPage to enter text, you will find that it is very similar to using Word. You can therefore format or emphasise the font, change its size and use the normal move or copy options. You can also colour the page background and flow the text round objects in different ways.

Each time you make changes, you can check what it would look like when published on the Web by viewing it in Preview. You can also check how the page will look in your browser. Ideally, check it in two different browsers as they can interpret the page in different ways.

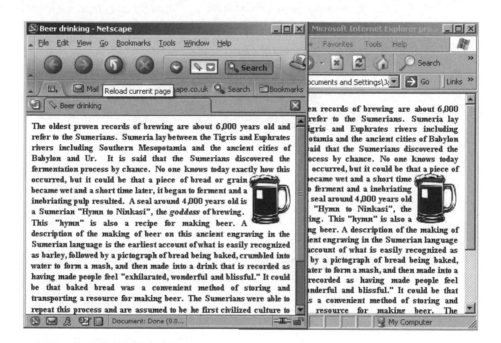

### 2.5.1 Previewing in FrontPage

1 *Click the Preview tab at the bottom of the page.*

2 *Return to editing view by clicking the Normal tab.*

### 2.5.2 Previewing in the Browser

1 *Click the Preview in Browser button on the toolbar* 🔲.

Or

2 *Click the File menu.*

3 *Click Preview in Browser.*

4 *Save any changes if asked to do so.*

5  If you have added pictures, they need to be saved separately and you will open a Save Embedded Files box.

6  Check that pictures are being saved in the same folder as the web page, or click Change Folder to browse for the folder.

7  Click OK.

8  Click to select a browser if more than one is installed on your computer.

9  Click in the resolution radio button if you want to view the page at a particular window size.

10  Click to save the page automatically if you will be carrying out a lot of editing and will want to keep previewing the latest changes.

11  Click Preview to open the page in your browser window.

## 2.5.3 Working with Browser and FrontPage Together

[1] *Return to FrontPage or the browser by clicking the button that will be minimised on the taskbar.*

Or

[2] *Hold **Alt** and press the **Tab** key until the application you want to open is selected. It will open when you let go of the keys.*

[3] *If you move between browser and FrontPage in this way, click the Refresh button on the browser toolbar to make sure you are viewing the latest version of the page.*

[4] *Click Save regularly to update the page in FrontPage.*

## 2.5.4 Formatting Text

**Assessment Objective 2g**

After typing your text, change its look just as you would when word processing. Use the formatting toolbar buttons and drop down lists to change selected text.

**1** *Apply a different font.*

**2** *Apply a different font size.*

**3** *Click to apply bold, underline or italic emphasis.*

**4** *Click the Increase Font Size or Decrease Font Size to change the font size in steps.*

**5** *Click to apply a colour to the text.*

**6** *Click to align text centrally, or to the right or left of the page.*

(See Chapter 1 (page **55**) for full details of formatting text.)

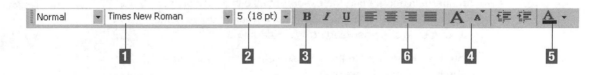

## 2.5.5 Font Sizes

One difference between FrontPage and Word is that text sizes are labelled differently: there are only seven sizes ranging from size 1–8 pt (very small) to size 7–36 pt (very large). These can be applied to different levels of text so that headings are the largest, subheadings are a smaller size and main text is the smallest size.

## 2.5.6 Using Styles

An alternative to setting the exact font size is to use styles. You can click the style box (showing Normal by default) and select a style such as Heading 1 or Heading 5.

Note that these work in the opposite direction to font sizes – the largest style is Heading 1.

## 2.6 Backgrounds

**Assessment Objective 2h** Web pages can have any type of background. They can be white, plain coloured, patterned or can use one or more images over which the text is positioned.

### 2.6.1 Applying a Background

1. *Right click the page and select Page Properties.*

Or

2. *Click the Format menu.*

3. *Click Background.*

4. *On the Background tab, click in the Colors – Background box.*

5. *Click a coloured box to apply that colour or click More Colors for a wider selection.*

6. *You can also change the colour of page or hyperlink text to make it stand out from the background.*

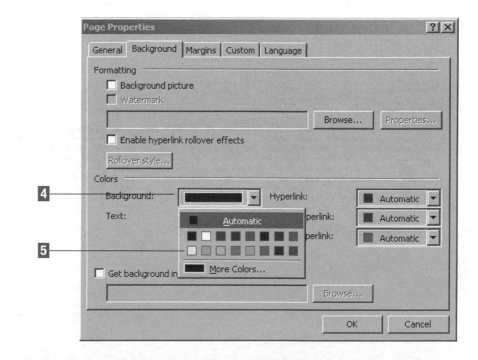

### I cannot find the background colour displayed in the code

Note that colours are visible on a printout in the form of hexadecimal codes such as #00FFFF. It will thus be evident if you have not applied a background colour.

## 2.7 Controlling Text Flow

**Assessment Objective 2i**

There are many ways that you can change the appearance of the page: you can wrap the text round images in different ways, or create a table so that the text appears in columns. Some web pages also use frames so that different page contents are visible in different areas of the page.

You will not be asked to do any of these for New CLAIT, but text wrap options are available from the Picture Properties box and you insert a table in a similar way to doing so in Word (explained in Chapter 1, page **000**).

Simple changes include using appropriate spaces between headings, subheadings and main text, and realigning the text.

## 2.7.1 Aligning Text

[1] *Select the text.*

[2] *Click an alignment button on the toolbar.*

**3** *Click Justify for a full block of text, to make the text edges neater.*

The oldest proven records of brewing are about 6,000 years old and refer to the Sumerians. Sumeria lay between the Tigris and Euphrates rivers including Southern Mesopotamia and the ancient cities of Babylon and Ur. It is said that the Sumerians discovered the fermentation process by chance. No one knows today exactly how this occurred, but it could be that a piece of bread or grain became wet and a short time later, it began to ferment and a inebriating pulp resulted. A seal around 4,000 years old is a Sumerian "Hymn to Ninkasi", the *goddess* of brewing. This "hymn" is also a recipe for making beer. A description of the making of beer on this ancient engraving in the Sumerian language is the earliest account of what is easily recognized as barley, followed by a pictograph of bread being baked, crumbled into water to form a mash, and then made into a drink that is recorded as having made people feel "exhilarated, wonderful and blissful." It could be that baked bread was a convenient method of storing and transporting a resource for making beer. The Sumerians were able to repeat this process and are assumed to be he first civilized culture to brew beer. They had discovered a "divine drink" which certainly was a gift from the gods.

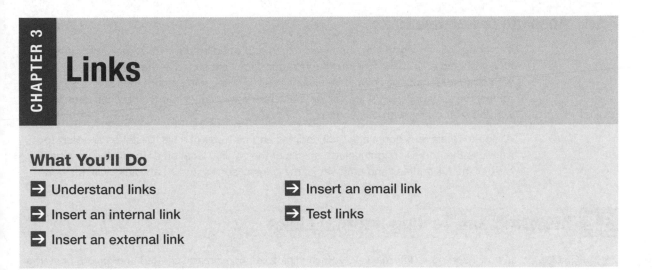

# CHAPTER 3

# Links

## What You'll Do

→ Understand links

→ Insert an internal link

→ Insert an external link

→ Insert an email link

→ Test links

## 3.1 | Understanding Web Page Links

3

Links are a common device to make navigating web pages and finding information much easier. They are called hyperlinks and can be text or graphics.

Each time you click a hyperlink when the mouse pointer displays a hand, embedded code directs the browser to open a relevant new page. This can be another page on the same website (or file on your computer if the website is not yet published on the Web) – an internal link; a different website page – an external link; or an email message window.

For example:

- A website index will be made up of internal links so that you can go straight to products, delivery charges, checkout or company background pages with one click.

- To view manufacturers' own pages, detailing more about products you want to buy, a shopping website might add external links to the websites of a range of different companies.

- To contact Customer Services or get technical help, you can click an email link and type your message straight away.

### 3.1.1  Absolute or Relative Links

The computer on which you store web pages published on the Web is generally referred to as a web server. If all the files making up your pages are stored in the same folder, links within the folder can be relative, referred to only by file name and not the full folder/directory pathway. If you move your folder of web pages to a different server, the files will still refer correctly to one another.

Absolute references contain the full address and pathway of a file. Mistakes are easy to make as the address might include details of the original location of the file on your hard disk or the full address and pathway of the original server, and so any links will not work.

## 3.2  Inserting and Testing Internal Links

**Assessment Objective 3a**

When inserting an internal link, you can link to a page already created and saved, or start a new one that you can then link to.

### 3.2.1  Inserting an Internal Link

1. *Type and then select the text you want as the clickable text, or select ready-made text. You can also select an image.*

2. *Click the Insert Hyperlink button.*

Or

3. *Right click the text or image.*

Or

4. *Click the Insert menu.*

5. *Click Hyperlink.*

6. *Check that the correct text is showing in the Text to display: box.*

7. *If the web page you want to link to is visible in the window, click its name.*

8. *Otherwise, browse for the file so that it shows in the Look in: box.*

9. *Click the file name. It will appear in the Address: box.*

10. *Click OK.*

11. *On the Preview tab in FrontPage, hyperlink text will show as blue and underlined.*

## 3.2.2 Testing a Link

[1] *On the Normal tab hold **Ctrl** and click the hyperlink text.*

Or

[2] *Right click and select Follow Hyperlink.*

[3] *The linked page should open on screen.*

[4] *Return to the original page by clicking its named tab.*

[5] *You can also test the link in the browser:*

[A] *Preview the page in your browser.*

[B] *Hover over the text and the linked page details should show in the bottom left hand corner of the page.*

[C] *Click the hyperlink.*

[D] *The linked page should open.*

[E] *Return to your original page by clicking the Back button.*

## 3.3 Inserting and Testing External Links

Assessment
Objective 3b If you know the full web page address, you can type it in. You can also go to the Web and search for the page. Its address will be inserted automatically.

### 3.3.1 Inserting an External Link

1. Select the text or image to act as the link.

2. Click the Insert Hyperlink button.

3. Type the full web page address into the Address box, including http://.

Or

4. Click the Browse the Web button to connect to the Web.

5. Search for the page you want to link to.

6. When it is open on screen, click the FrontPage button on the taskbar to re-open the Insert Hyperlink box.

7. The full address of the visited page will have been added to the Address box.

8. Click OK.

### 3.3.2 Testing an External Link

1. Preview the page in your browser. Make sure you are connected to the Internet.

2. Click the hyperlink text.

3. The correct web page should open.

4. Return to your page by clicking the Back button.

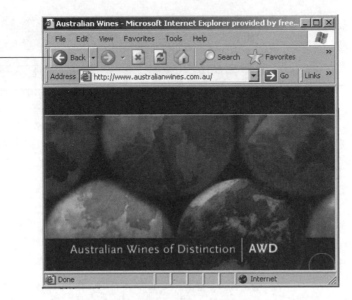

Source: Permission from Southcorp Wines Pty Ltd

## 3.4 Inserting and Testing Email Links

**Assessment
Objective 3c**

For these to work your machine must be set up with an email system.

### 3.4.1 Inserting an Email Link

1. *Select the text or graphic to be clicked.*

2. *Open the Insert Hyperlink window.*

3. *Click the E-mail Address button.*

4. *Click in the E-Mail address: box and type the full address. The text mailto: will appear automatically, to tell the browser that it is an email link.*

5. *If you want an entry in the subject box of the message completed each time, enter suitable text in the Subject box.*

6. *Click OK.*

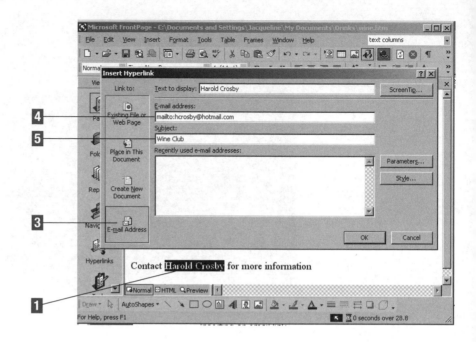

## 3.4.2  Testing an Email Link

1. *Click to move to the Preview tab.*

2. *Click the email link text.*

3. *Your email system should open and a message should appear with the To: and Subject: boxes already completed.*

## 3.5  Editing or Removing Hyperlinks

You can delete a hyperlink if you make a mistake or edit it if any of the details change.

## 3.5.1  Removing a Link

1. *Right click the text.*

2. *Click Hyperlink Properties to open the Edit Hyperlink box.*

3. *Click Remove Hyperlink.*

4. *Click OK.*

## 3.5.2  Editing a Link

1. *Open the Hyperlink box as above.*

2. *Retype any entries in the boxes that have changed or are incorrect.*

3. *Click OK.*

When you click the HTML tab, you see the underlying code that has been written as you created the page. Blue text is the code and black text is the entry. If you take care not to change any codes or punctuation symbols, you should find you can edit entries on this tab.

Links look like this:

<a href="http://www.australianwines.com.au">Australia< /a>

- ■ <a href= introduces the link.
- ■ /a> ends the link.
- ■ The text in quotation marks is the page, web or email address.
- ■ The text after the bracket is the clickable text.

You can see three links on the page:

1 Internal link to a different page on the computer.

2 External link to a website.

3 An email address that is being changed.

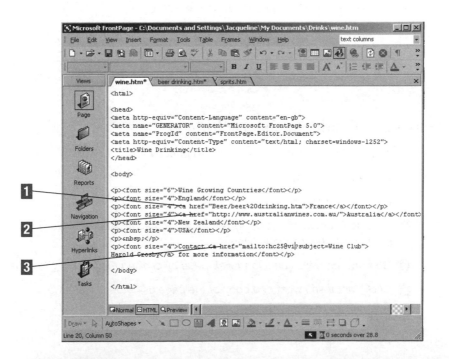

# CHAPTER 4

# Printing

## What You'll Do

→ Print web pages from FrontPage

→ Print web pages from a browser

→ Print HTML source code

## 4.1 Printing a Web Page

**Assessment Objective 4a**

You can print a Normal view of your page or the HTML code from FrontPage. You can also print different views of your page from the browser.

 **Critical Error**
Missing printouts.

### 4.1.1 Previewing in FrontPage Before Printing

1. Click the tab for the view you want to print: Normal or HTML.

2. Click the File menu.

3. Click Print Preview.

4. Use the Zoom In or Out buttons to change magnification, or click on the page. The pointer will show a magnifying glass.

5. Go between pages on a long web page by clicking the Next or Previous page buttons.

6. Click Print if you want one copy of the page using default settings.

7. Click Close to leave Print Preview.

## 4.1.2 Printing from FrontPage

1. *Click the Normal tab.*

2. *Click File.*

3. *Click Print.*

4. *Change any settings such as page or copy numbers if you want to print anything other than a single copy of one web page.*

5. *Click Print.*

## 4.1.3 Printing from a Web Browser

1. *Preview the page in your browser.*

2. *Click the Print button* *.*

## 4.1.4 Headers and Footers

For New CLAIT, you need to show the file folder and pathway location when printing from a browser. Add them if they are not displayed.

[1] Click File.

[2] Click Page Setup.

[3] Add '&u' into the Header box. ('&w' displays the page title.)

[4] Click OK.

**[3]**

## 4.2 Printing the HTML Source Code

Assessment Objective 4b

In FrontPage, printing the code requires you to click the HTML tab before printing normally so that the code is displayed. You need to reveal the code if you want to print it from the browser.

### 4.2.1 Printing HTML Code from FrontPage

[1] Open the page you want to print.

[2] Click the HTML tab to reveal the code.

[3] Click the Print button.

## 4.2.2 Printing Source Code from a Browser

1. *Open the page in your browser.*

2. *Click the View menu.*

3. *Click Source.*

4. *This opens a window in Notepad revealing the HTML code.*

5. *Click the File menu.*

6. *Click Print.*

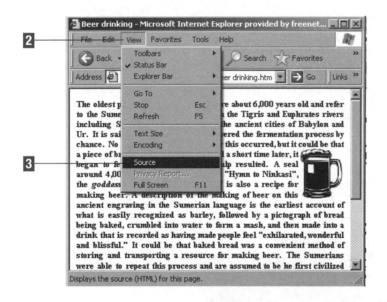

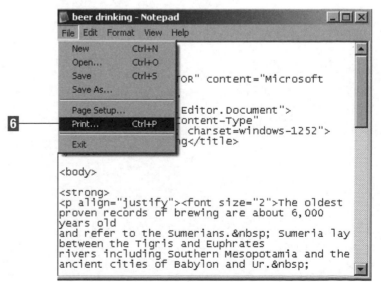

## Learning outcomes

At the end of this unit, you should be able to:

→ Identify and use email and browsing software

→ Navigate the World Wide Web and use search techniques to locate data on the web

→ Transmit and receive email messages and attachments

# CHAPTER 1

# Communication Software

**1**

## What You'll Do

→ Discover the Internet

→ Understand how email works

→ Understand email addresses

→ Identify the appropriate software for using email

→ Know the rules of using email

→ Use antivirus software

## 1.1 The Internet

**Assessment Objective 1**

Being part of the networks of computers that make up the Internet will enable you to use your computer to communicate with others wherever they are in the world. You can download pages of information – web pages – onto your computer, publish your own pages for others to access and send and receive electronic messages – emails.

To use the Internet fully, you need:

- Browser software for viewing web pages.

- A connection to the Internet, normally via the telephone network.

- An Internet Service Provider (ISP) for your dial-up or broadband connection.

- Email software for creating and reading messages.

## 1.2 How Email Works

### 1.2.1 Email Addresses

Your email address is the equivalent of a telephone number as it allows other people to contact you over the network. It is made up of your username, the @ symbol and the address of your ISP's mail server – a special computer handling emails.

An example of a typical address is:

jackie.sherman (username)
@
hotmail.com (server)

written as jackie.sherman@hotmail.com

## 1.2.2 Software Needed to Use Email

There are two different types of email program you can use:

- Software installed on your own computer such as Outlook Express, Outlook, Eudora or FirstClass. (This chapter uses Microsoft Outlook for the examples.)

- Web-based services provided by sites such as www.yahoo.co.uk, www.hotmail.com or www.postmaster.co.uk.

The main difference between them is that, for web-based mail, travellers had the advantage of being able to access emails away from home as long as they could get onto the Internet. Nowadays, even if you regularly use Outlook or Outlook Express, you should also be able to access your messages on your ISP's server.

## 1.3 Netiquette

**Assessment Objective 1b**

Sending emails, even personal ones, should take account of normal rules of behaviour so that you do not cause offence or inconvenience other people. As an employee you will have certain responsibilities when using this form of communication and may have to sign an agreement before you are given an email address.

General rules of behaviour, particularly applicable to posting messages to special interest groups (usergroups), are known as *netiquette*.

Some of the most common include:

- Being very careful that 'jokes' are not misunderstood.

- Never libelling another person.

- Avoiding over-use of capital letters (known as SHOUTING).

- Cutting back on continuously re-quoting earlier messages, so that emails do not become too long.

- Not sending 'spam' or the equivalent of junk mail.

- Always attributing quotes or authorship of material.

## 1.4 Virus Checking

### 1.4.1 Why Use a Virus Checker?

**Assessment Objective 1c**

A virus is a program specifically written to infect computers and cause damage. They can cause your email system to send endless, meaningless messages to everyone in your address book; slow down your computer; delete files or keep closing your machine down before you can save your work. With the number of such malicious programs being written today, it is vital that everyone protects their computer against infection. College or company computers will have virus checking software installed, but personal computers should also be protected.

### 1.4.2 Anti-Virus Programs

Appropriate programs can be bought and installed from CD or downloaded from the Internet. There are free or time-limited demo programs available such as AVG, Panda or BitDefender, or you can buy more sophisticated anti-virus software produced by companies such as MacAfee, Norton and Sophos.

### 1.4.3 Using the Software

[1] *Hover the mouse over the taskbar icon to see a screen tip detailing the software.*

[2] *Double click the icon to open the software.*

[3] *Select a scan – you could check a removable storage disk or your entire system.*

Or

[4] *Right click a drive on the desktop.*

[5] *Click the Scan for Viruses option.*

[6] *A window will appear showing your files being checked.*

[7] *If any viruses are found, they will be removed or quarantined so they cannot do any harm.*

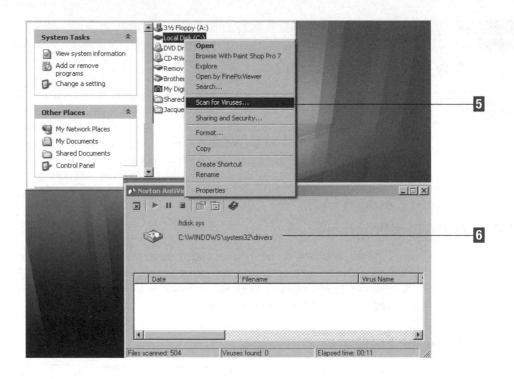

# CHAPTER 2

# The World Wide Web

## What You'll Do

→ Discover the World Wide Web

→ Discover web pages

→ Navigate the World Wide Web

→ Understand URLs

→ Use local search facilities

→ Use search engines

→ Find specific data

→ Save web pages

→ Bookmark web addresses

→ Print web pages

**2**

## 2.1 What is the World Wide Web?

All the multimedia pages of text, images, sounds and videos published over the Internet that can be viewed when using a browser are known collectively as the World Wide Web.

## 2.2 Using a Browser to View Web Pages

Browsers are either installed when you buy a computer or downloaded from the Internet. The four most common are: Internet Explorer, Netscape, Firefox and Opera. You can have more than one on your computer as they offer slightly different facilities and web pages may look different. The examples for this chapter are taken from Internet Explorer.

### 2.2.1 Launching a Browser

Double click the browser icon on your computer desktop. It may have the browser name, or that of your Internet Service Provider.

Internet
Explorer

## 2.2.2 The Browser Toolbar

The browser toolbar visible when viewing web pages offers a range of toolbar buttons for carrying out the main activities you are likely to perform. Some will open menus on screen when you click them.

**1** *Back button* – click to move back to a page opened previously.

**2** *Forward* – move forward to a page you have returned from.

**3** *Stop* – cancel downloading a page.

**4** *Refresh* – load the page again, usually to make sure you have the latest version.

**5** *Home* – open the page that always starts a web session.

**6** *Search* – use the default search facilities.

**7** *Favorites* – save a link to the URL of a page you may want to revisit.

**8** *History* – find a page you have visited in the past.

**9** *Print* – print the current web page.

**10** *Address box* – shows the address of the current page, or you can type in one you want to view.

**11** *Go button* – click to open the page whose address has been entered into the Address box.

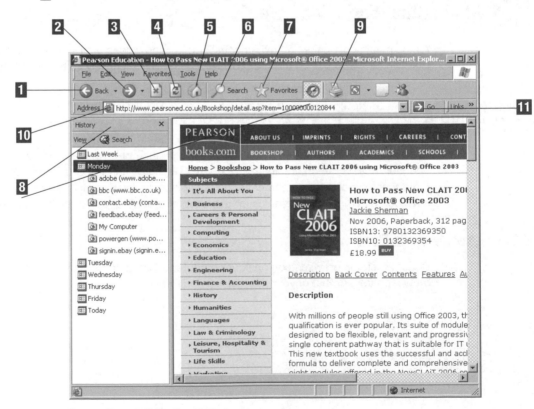

Source: Pearson Education Limited

## 2.3 Navigating Web Pages

There are two different ways to open a new web page:

- *Use the Address box*.

- *Click a hyperlink*.

### 2.3.1 Understanding URLs

**Assessment Objective 2a** Every web page has a unique address where it can be found. This is its URL – Uniform Resource Locator. The addresses are in a standard form so that they are easy to work with. One example of the URL of a welcome page on a website is:

http://www.pearsoned.com

### 2.3.2 Parts of a URL

- **http://** – This stands for HyperText Transfer Protocol, showing that it meets the requirements for pages published on the Web.

- **www** – This stands for World Wide Web.

- **pearsoned.com** – This is the name of the computer housing the page, referred to as the *domain name*.

Often the domain name is followed by forward slashes and other entries. These show the exact folder location of an individual page.

http://www.pearsoned.com/community/index.htm

### 2.3.3 Domain Names

These normally start with the company or organisation name and then indicate what type of organisation they are and where they are located in the world.

| NAME | ACTIVITY | LOCATION |
| --- | --- | --- |
| Microsoft.com | Company | International |
| Pearsoned.co.uk | Company | UK |
| Bristol.ac.uk | Education | UK |
| Washington.edu | Education | USA |
| Unimelb.edu.au | Education | Australia |
| Derby.gov.uk | Local/national government | UK |
| Ageconcern.org.uk | Charity | UK |

Some UK organisations may have **com** rather than **co.uk** domain names, but if you type **co.uk** you will often be redirected to the correct website automatically.

### 2.3.4  Guessing a URL

If you want to visit the website of the UK computer manufacturer Dell, or the University of Michigan, USA, you should be able to guess the URL by asking:

1. *What is the name of the organisation?*

2. *What main activity is it involved in?*

3. *Where is it based?*

### 2.3.5  Using the URL to Open a Web Page

1. *Click in the Address box. The current entry will turn blue.*

2. *Start typing the URL. You do not need to start with **http://** as this is added automatically.*

3. *If you have visited the same page before, typing the domain name may bring up the full URL. Otherwise start with **www**.*

4. *Click Go or press Enter.*

### 2.3.6  Using Hyperlinks to Open a Web Page

**Assessment Objective 2b**

1. *Move the pointer over a web page.*

2. *When it shows a hand, click once.*

3. *The new page will open.*

4. *To keep the original page open on screen, right click and select Open in New Window.*

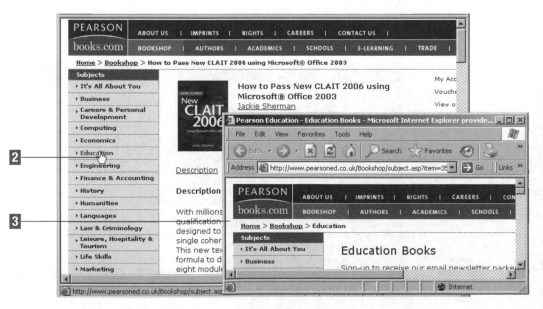

Source: Pearson Education Limited

### 2.3.7 Navigating Around a Web Page

1. *Scroll down or across the page to view information not visible on the screen. Either click an arrow or drag the grey box in the scroll bar, or drag the central scroll wheel on top of your mouse.*

2. *Click a labelled button that makes up an index.*

3. *Click any text, image or other part of the screen when the pointer shows a hand.*

4. *Some pages have a hyperlink to different parts of the same page built into them. For example, click a link to return to the top of the page after reading a large block of text.*

## 2.4 Searching for Information

To find out if a company sells a particular product, what plants are in your local garden centre or how much it costs to go on the London Eye, it is likely that searching the organisation's own website will provide you with the answers.

If you want to know where you can still see *Lord of the Rings*, how much engagement rings are likely to cost, who has a canal boat holiday available in April or whether you have spelt 'onomatopoeia' correctly, the answer could be anywhere.

Websites set up to provide answers to general questions are known as search engines. There are many search engines you can use, including:

www.google.co.uk

http://uk.yahoo.com

www.ask.com

www.live.com

www.gigablast.com

**Critical Error**
Failing to locate the correct page.

### 2.4.1 Using Local Search Facilities

**Assessment Objective 2c**

1. *Type the URL of the organisation such as www.pearsoned.co.uk/bookshop into the Address box and press Enter.*

2. *You may need to type your query or a keyword into the search box provided.*

3. *Scan the page for an appropriate link to the information you are seeking. For IT books, for example, you could click Computing.*

4. *Work down through further hyperlinks if necessary until you find the information.*

Source: Pearson Education Limited

## 2.4.2 Using Search Engines

Assessment
Objective 2d

**1** *Type the URL of the search engine into the Address box and press Enter.*

**2** *When the page opens, enter as much detail about your query as you can into the search box.*

**3** *To look for images, maps or news items, you can click a separate hyperlink. Otherwise you will be searching for relevant web pages.*

**4** *Click a checkbox to limit the search to UK sites.*

**5** *To start the search, click the button under or to the right of the box – it may be labelled 'Go', 'Search' etc. or display a magnifying glass.*

**6** *Web pages containing your keywords will be listed.*

**7** *You will also see an indication of the number of pages found.*

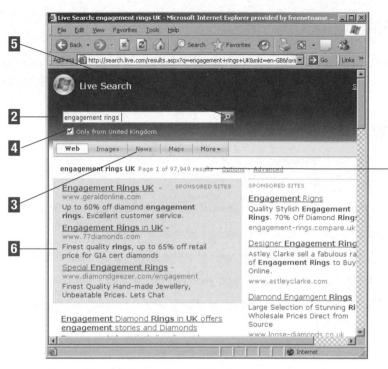

Source: Microsoft Corporation and Live Search

## 2.4.3 Finding Specific Data

**Assessment Objective 2e**

1. *Scroll down the search list until you see an appropriate web page listed.*

2. *Search results will be listed 10–15 to a page. Click a page number or Next button at the bottom of the page to scroll through the next set of web pages.*

3. *Read the brief description under each one to check that it is worth visiting.*

4. *Click the blue, underlined text.*

5. *When the page opens, scan for the information you are seeking.*

6. *If it is not there, click the Back button to return to the search list and visit another web page.*

7. *If the page has too much text, click the Edit menu.*

8. *Click Find (on this page).*

9. *Type your keywords into the box.*

10. *Click Find Next.*

11. *Keep clicking the button until the section you want to read is highlighted.*

### I haven't saved the right information!

A common mistake is to save and print the search list on the search engine page, rather than an actual web page containing the relevant information.

## 2.5 Saving Data

Assessment Objective 2f A web page is a combination of files such as image files, banners, backgrounds and text. You can save individual parts, a combined page or the complete page including separate files.

### 2.5.1 Saving a Web Page

1. *Click the File menu.*

2. *Click Save As.*

3. *In the Save Web Page box, select the type of save you want to make:*

   A *Web page, complete saves all associated files.*

   B *Web Archive saves a snapshot of the current page as a single file.*

   C *HTML saves the information without graphics or sound files.*

   D *Text File saves the text content only, without layout and formatting, and will reopen in Notepad.*

4. *Rename the file if necessary.*

5. *Click the Save button.*

**6** *If you pick a complete web page save, you will see details of all the files from the page being saved separately.*

Source: www.boardgamegeek.com

You could also hold **Ctrl** and press **S** to save the file as a complete web page.

## 2.5.2 Saving an Image

**1** *Right click an image.*

**2** *Click Save Picture As.*

Or

**3** *Click the Save button that may appear on a small toolbar at the top of the picture.*

**4** *In the Save as type: box, leave the type of image file as it appears. It will normally be a JPEG or GIF file.*

**5** *Browse for a suitable location so that it shows in the Save in: box.*

**6** *Rename the file if the title is not clear. (Many pictures have obscure numbers instead of clear names.)*

**7** *Click Save.*

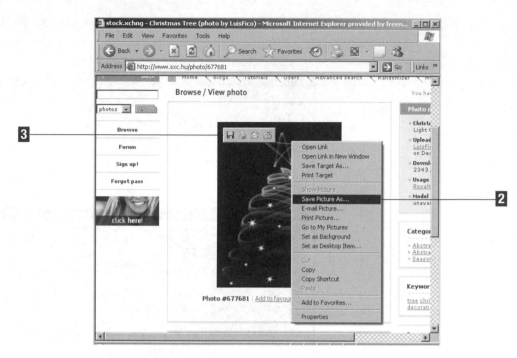

Source: Permission from Dr Luis Francisco Cordero for Christmas tree photo, as featured on www.sxc.hu

**Critical Error**
Failing to save the specified image from the web page in the format required.

## 2.6 Bookmarking a Page

**Assessment Objective 2g**

Going backwards and forwards between web pages can be confusing and it is very difficult to remember every page you might wish to revisit. Instead, you can bookmark the URL of any page of interest and store it in a folder. To revisit the page, click the name and it will open on screen.

In Internet Explorer, bookmarked pages are stored in a Favorites folder.

### 2.6.1 Adding a URL to Favorites

1. *Make sure the page is open in your browser.*

2. *Click the Favorites toolbar button to open a list of bookmarked pages in a separate pane.*

3. *Click the Favorites menu to open the list on screen.*

   A. *Yellow folders contain bookmarked pages.*

   B. *The blue IE icon shows pages that were added to the list but not placed in a folder.*

4. *Click Add to Favorites.*

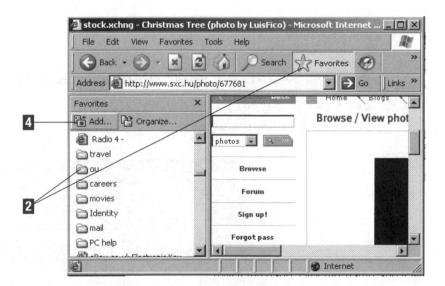

5. *Rename the page title if it will be clearer for later use.*

6. *Click Create in if no folders are visible.*

7. *Click a current folder in which to store the URL.*

8. *If no folder is suitable, click New Folder and create a folder in which to store the page.*

9. *Click OK.*

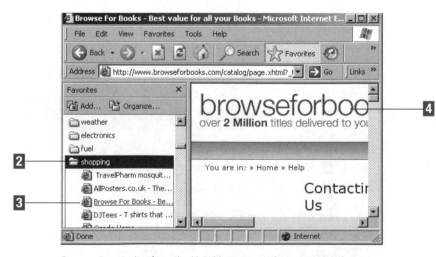

A shortcut to adding a URL to the bottom of the Favorites list is to hold **Ctrl** and press **D**.

## 2.6.2 Opening a Favorite

1 *Open the Favorites list.*

2 *Click the folder containing the URL of the page you want to view.*

3 *Click the page name.*

4 *The page will open on screen.*

Source: Permission from the Hub Management for screenshot from
www.browseforbooks.com

## 2.7 Organising Bookmarked Pages

There are two ways you can organise favourites, using the menu or on screen.

### 2.7.1 Using the Organize Favorites Window

1. *Open the Favorites list.*

2. *Click Organize.*

3. *In the right hand pane, scroll down the list. If the target page is in a folder, click to open it.*

4. *Click the page name.*

5. *Click one of the buttons to rename, delete or move the URL or create a new folder.*

## 2.7.2 Organising Favorites on Screen

1. *Click to open the Favorites list.*

2. *Right click any bookmarked page and select delete or rename from the menu that will appear.*

3. *Click and drag a favourite to move it into a different folder. Its position will be shown by a black horizontal line. When the folder turns blue and opens, let go and it will drop into place.*

4. *Drag a favourite to a new position in the list.*

## 2.8  Printing Web Pages

**Assessment Objective 2h**

Web pages are not the same as document pages and so a single web page may extend across a number of sheets of paper when printed. They may also not print exactly as they appear: in portrait orientation some parts visible on screen may be truncated. Check in Print Preview before printing, to make sure you know what will print out.

 **Critical Error**
Missing printouts.

## 2.8.1 Checking a Printout

1. *Click the File menu.*

2. *Click Print Preview.*

3. *Check the number of pages that will print.*

4. *Check that all data is visible.*

5. *Click Close.*

 **What do I do if the page doesn't print out properly?**

Correct errors before printing in two ways: change to landscape orientation to display the full width of the page, and set the printer to print page 1 only, if you want just the first part of the web page entry.

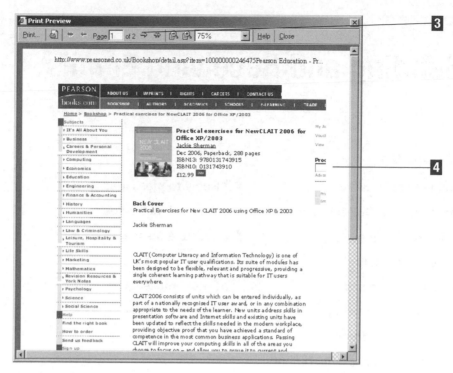

Source: Pearson Education Limited

## 2.8.2 Printing

1 *Click the Print button on the browser to print a single copy of the entire web page using default settings.*

Or

2 *Click the File menu.*

3 *Click Print.*

4 *Click in the Page Range box to limit printing to a particular number of pages.*

5 *Amend the Number of Copies if you want to print more than one.*

6 *Click Print.*

---

### ⊗ Critical Error
Failing to print the correct page.

---

### Can I take a screen print of the information instead?

When taking a New CLAIT assessment, a screen print of a web page is not acceptable.

# CHAPTER 3

# Sending and Receiving Emails

## What You'll Do

→ Launch Outlook

→ Understand the Outlook layout

→ Receive messages

→ Access attachments

→ Attach files to emails

→ Store an email address

→ Recall a stored address

→ Store messages and attachments

→ Reply to messages

→ Forward messages

→ Create a message

→ Copy messages

→ Delete messages

→ Print messages

→ Print attachments

## 3.1 Launching Outlook

1. *Click the Start button.*

2. *Click All Programs.*

3. *Click Microsoft Outlook.*

Or

4. *Click a shortcut to the program on the desktop.*

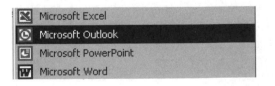

**How Outlook is Organised**

Outlook is an office management program, integrating email with a calendar, a reminder system and time and task planners.

For New CLAIT, you need to be able to use just two parts of the system: the email folders and the address book, referred to as Contacts.

## 3.2.1 The Outlook Screen

When Outlook opens, it is divided into a number of panes and you can decide which ones you view.

**1** The Outlook Bar houses shortcuts to the main parts of the system.

**2** The Folder list is a complete list of the various parts you will work with.

**3** The main window reveals the contents of any selected folder.

**4** *To add or close a pane*:

  **A** *Click the View menu.*

  **B** *Click the named pane to add or remove a tick.*

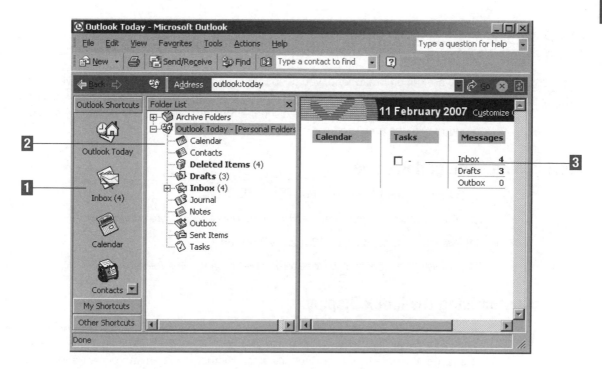

### 3.2.2 Folders

Folders containing items you have not checked will be bold and will show the number of items in brackets. The role of the folders is as follows:

1. *Inbox* – contains all messages that have been received.

2. *Outbox* – contains messages waiting to be sent.

3. *Sent Items* – contains copies of messages that have been sent.

4. *Drafts* – contains saved messages you are still working on.

5. *Contacts* – contains names, addresses and other details of people you write to or who have written to you.

6. *Outlook Today* – your system may be set to open in this view which summarises this week's meetings, tasks and messages.

## 3.3 Exiting Outlook

1. *Click the Close button in the top right hand corner of the screen.*

2. *You may be reminded that you still have messages to send.*

## 3.4 Sending and Receiving Messages

**Assessment Objective 3a**

If you are not on broadband, you need to dial up to connect to the Internet when sending or receiving emails. To limit the amount of time spent online, do this only when you are ready to send several messages. Always disconnect before reading, composing or otherwise working with the email software.

### 3.4.1 Using Send and Receive

1. *Click the Send/Receive button* [Send/Receive] .

2. *Emails stored on your mail server will be downloaded into your Inbox.*

3. *Messages waiting in your Outbox will be sent.*

4. *Copies of sent emails will be stored in your Sent Items folder.*

### 3.4.2 Customising the Inbox Display

Incoming messages will be identified in a variety of ways, depending on how the system has been set up. For example, you can choose to view the sender, the subject of the message, the date it was received, its size, whether it has an attachment and if it has a high priority.

**1** *Right click any heading such as From or Subject.*

Or

**2** *Click the View menu.*

**3** *Click Customize Current View.*

**4** *Click Show Fields.*

**5** *Click any category in the left pane and click Add to add it as a heading.*

**6** *Click any unwanted fields and click Remove.*

**7** *Change the order of headings by clicking the Move Up or Down buttons.*

**8** *Click OK.*

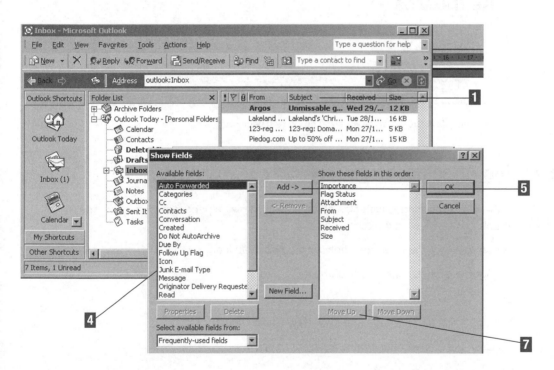

## 3.4.3 Reading Emails

**1** Double click an email showing in the Inbox. It will open in its own window.

**2** Click the Next button to work through the messages.

**3** If you have a preview pane open, read the selected message here.

**4** If you have set the option to AutoPreview, read short details of the message under the subject information.

**5** Click the Close button to close the message window and return to the main Outlook window.

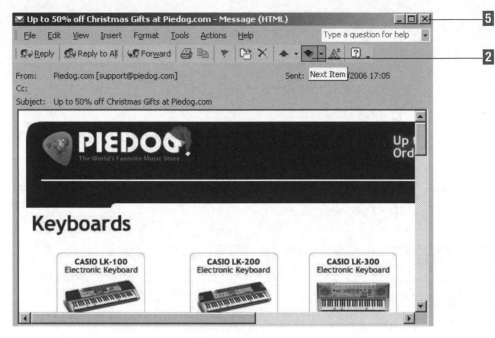

Source: ©Visualsoft UK Ltd, www.visualsoft.co.uk, with permission

## 3.5 Accessing Attachments

Assessment Objective 3b

In the Inbox, messages with files attached will display a paperclip icon. Open the attachment to view its contents.

**1** *Double click the message showing the paperclip icon.*

**2** *Double click the named attachment.*

Or

**3** *Right click the message and click View Attachments.*

**4** *Click the named attachment you want to open.*

Or

**5** *Right click the attachment showing in the preview pane and click Open.*

**6** *If necessary, take the advice to save it first, rather than open it directly.*

![i] **How careful should I be?**

Viruses are often spread in attachments, so either delete any suspicious messages without opening or save the attachment and run a virus check before opening.

## 3.6 Attaching Files

**Assessment Objective 3c**

When you want to send someone a map, picture or other electronic file, attach it to a message. Take care that the attachment is:

- Not too big. It will take far too long to send or download onto your recipient's machine.

- Created in software that they are likely to have on their computer, so that they can open and read the file.

### 3.6.1 Attaching a File to a Message

1. *Create the message as normal (see page 325).*

2. *Click the Attach File button.*

Or

3. *Click the Insert menu.*

4. *Click File Attachment.*

5. *Browse for the file on your computer.*

6. *Click its name.*

7. *Click Insert.*

8  *Repeat to send more than one attachment.*

9  *An Attach box will open in the message showing the attached file(s).*

10  *Send the message and its attachment will be sent at the same time.*

```
New invention - Message (Plain Text)                              _ □ ×

 File   Edit   View   Insert   Format   Tools   Actions   Help      Type a question for help  ▼

 ⊠ Send   🖉   !   »              ▼        ▼  A  B  I  U  ≡ ≡ ≡ ⋮≡  »

  To...     pwatson@gadjets.co.uk

  Cc...

 Subject:   New invention

 Attach...  🔟 Door opening.doc (10 KB)

 Pete

 I am sending you a copy of my latest invention, a unique door
 opener, so that you can give me your opinion.

 Look forward to your comments

 J
```

> ⊗ **Critical Error**
> Failing to attach the specified file, or attaching the wrong file.

## 3.7  Using an Address Book

You can automatically add the email address of anyone who writes to you to your list of contacts, or you can create a new entry if you are given the address.

Once you have addresses in your Contacts folder, add them directly to your messages rather than typing them out each time.

### 3.7.1  Storing Email Addresses

**Assessment Objective 3d**

1  *Click the Contacts folder.*

2  *Click the New button.*

**3** Complete as many boxes as you can/want to. You must include a display name and full email address.

**4** Click Save and Close to save the address.

**5** If you have the Phone List view set, you can enter the address details into the top empty box.

**6** Double click the entry to open the Contact window if you want to add or amend any details.

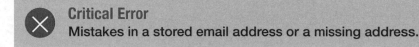

**Critical Error**

Mistakes in a stored email address or a missing address.

## 3.7.2 Storing an Address from Incoming Messages

1 *Right click the From header details.*

2 *Click Add to Contacts.*

3 *In the Contacts box, add or amend any details.*

4 *Click Save and Close.*

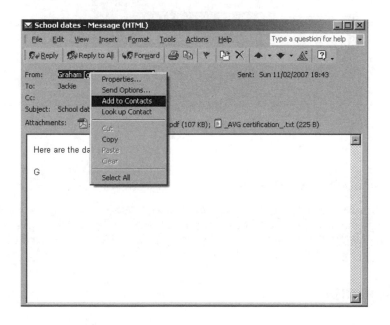

## 3.7.3 Recalling a Stored Address

Assessment
Objective 3e

1 *Start creating a message.*

2 *Click the To: or Cc: box.*

3 *Scroll through the names of your contacts in the Select Names box.*

4 *For a long list of names, type part of their name in the box to move directly to that section of the alphabetical list.*

5 *Click a name.*

6 *Click the button to add it to the To or Cc box.*

7 *Repeat if necessary to add further names.*

8 *Click OK to return to the message and continue composing.*

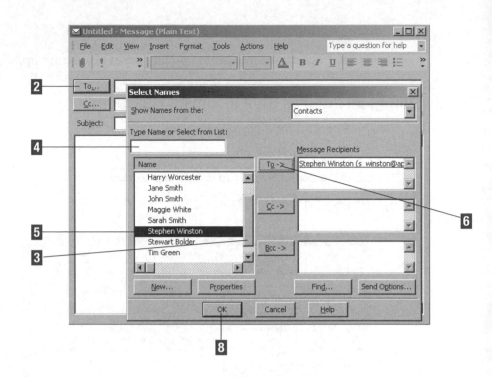

## I cannot find my contacts

If you work in an organisation with global address lists on computer, you may need to change the details in the Show Names from the: box to display the correct address list details.

# 3.8 Storing Messages

**Assessment Objective 3f**

Emails that you receive in the Inbox will remain there and start to build up. After a time, you may have too many to cope with. File them by grouping them into folders.

Even after filing emails carefully, you may still lose track of an important message. Use the find facilities to locate it.

## 3.8.1 Creating Folders

1. *Click the Inbox.*

2. *Click the File menu.*

3. *Click New.*

4. *Click Folder.*

Or

⑤ *Right click and click New Folder.*

⑥ *Name the new folder that will appear.*

## 3.8.2 Moving Messages into Folders

① *Select the message you want to move.*

② *To move several at once:*

  Ⓐ *Hold Shift as you click the last message to select a range of messages.*

  Ⓑ *Hold **Ctrl** to select individual messages.*

③ *Right click the selected message(s) and click Move to Folder.*

④ *Select a named new folder you have created.*

⑤ *Click Move.*

Or

**6** *Drag the selected message(s) across from the right hand pane to the new folder in the left hand pane when the pointer shows a white arrow.*

⑦ *Let go of the mouse and they will drop inside.*

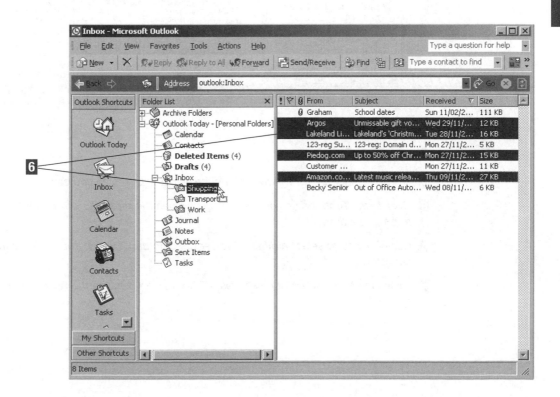

## 3.8.3 Finding Messages

**1** *Click the Find button.*

**2** *Enter part or all of the subject of the message.*

**3** *Enter the name of the correct folder location.*

**4** *Click Find Now.*

**5** *The message, if located, will be displayed in the window.*

**6** *Click Clear to see all your messages again.*

**7** *Click Options – Advanced Find to carry out a more detailed search.*

**8** *In the Advanced Find window, complete as many boxes as you can.*

**9** *Click in the Time: box if you know roughly when the message was received and click the appropriate time.*

**10** *Click Browse to select a different folder or subfolder in which you think the message was stored.*

**11** *Click Find Now. Relevant messages will be displayed below the Advanced Find window.*

## 3.8.4 Storing Attachments

If you open an attachment you have been sent, save it like any other file. You can also save attachments outside Outlook without actually opening them first. As noted earlier, you may be warned about opening an attachment and offered the chance to save it to disk anyway.

1. *Open the email.*

2. *Right click the attachment name and click Save As.*

Or

3. *Open the attachment.*

4. *Click File.*

5. *Click Save As.*

6. *Name and save the file as normal.*

Or

7. *Select but do not open the message.*

8. *Click File.*

9. *Click Save Attachments.*

10. *Click a named attachment or, if there are several, All Attachments.*

11. *In the Save All Attachments box, deselect any attachment you do not want to include in the save.*

12. *In the Save Attachment box, select a folder on your computer in which to save the attachment and complete the save as normal.*

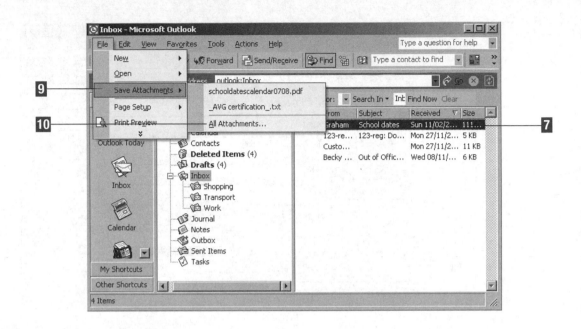

## 3.9 Replying to Messages

**Assessment Objective 3g**

When messages arrive in your Inbox, you can reply without typing in all the details. Bear in mind that, as you reply and send messages to the same person, the original text of previous messages will be included. This can make the final messages very long, so delete this 'message string' unless it is important for people to read all the details each time.

### 3.9.1 Replying

**1** *Click the message in the Inbox window.*

**2** *Click the Reply button to reply to the author of the message.*

**3** *Click Reply to All to send your reply to everyone who received a copy of the email.*

**4** *When the message box opens, the author's details will have been added to the To: box. When replying to all, everyone else's email address will have been added to the Cc: box.*

**5** *The subject of the message will have been added to the Subject box, preceded by RE: to show it is a reply.*

**6** *The content of the message will be displayed in the main window. Leave this if you want recipients to have a reminder of the message they sent. Otherwise, select and delete part or all of the text.*

**7** *Enter your reply text in the space above the original message.*

**8** *Click Send to send the email.*

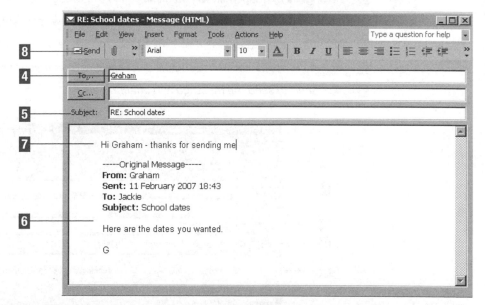

### When I reply, will I be sending back attachments?

In Outlook, any attachments that were sent with the original message will not be attached to a reply automatically, as replies do not normally require attachments sent back to the sender.

### Critical Error
Replying to the wrong message.

## 3.10 Forwarding Messages

Assessment
Objective 3h

You often want to send a message on to a third person, as it may contain information relevant to them. You may also want to send on an attachment you received. Forwarded messages include attachments automatically, so you will need to delete them if you do *not* want the recipient to have them.

### 3.10.1 Forwarding

1. *Click the message you received in the Inbox.*

2. *Click the Forward button* [Forward] .

3. *When the message window opens, the subject box will contain the original subject preceded by FW: to show it is a forwarded message.*

4. *Any attachments will be shown in the Attach box.*

5. *The original message text will be displayed in the window.*

6. *Click in the To: box to add the email address of the new recipient.*

7. *Add other email addresses if you want them to receive a copy of the message as well.*

8. *Click in the space above the original message text to add your own comments.*

9. *Click Send to send the message and attachments.*

**Critical Error**
A forwarded message that does not display the original message text unamended, or any attachments.

## 3.11 Creating a Message

**Assessment Objective 3i**

Emails have a standard format.

1. *The To: box containing the full email address of the recipient of the message.*

2. *The Cc: box containing email addresses for anyone you want to receive a copy.*

3. *The Subject box containing a brief summary of the content of the message.*

4. *The main message window containing the text of your message.*

### Can I make the odd mistake in an address?

No! Any inaccuracies, even with a full stop or underline, will mean the message cannot be sent. But you can use either upper or lower case.

## 3.11.1 Composing Messages

1. *With an email folder selected in the folder list, click the New button* New .

2. *If you have selected a different folder, click the drop down arrow next to the New button and click New Mail Message.*

3. *This opens the new message window.*

4. *Click in the To: box and enter the address of the message recipient.*

Or

5. *Recall a stored email by clicking the To: button.*

6. *Click in the Cc: box and enter further email addresses if sending copies.*

7. *Click in the Subject box and type a subject.*

8. *Click in the main window and type the message text.*

9. *Check the message for inaccuracies and spelling mistakes:*

   A. *Click Tools.*

   B. *Click Spelling.*

   C. *Work through the document, editing or ignoring suggested errors.*

10. *Click Send to place a copy of the message in the Outbox.*

11. *Your system may send the message automatically, or you can click the Send/Receive button on the main toolbar.*

**10** / **4** / **6** / **7** / **8**

```
New Pair of Shoes - Message (Plain Text)                          _ □ ×
 File  Edit  View  Insert  Format  Tools  Actions  Help     Type a question for help  ▼
 Send  ⫶  »                    ▼         ▼  A  B  I  U  ≡ ≡ ≡ ≣ ≣ ⫶⫶ ⫶⫶  »

  To...    gordon.whales@shoemaker.com
  Cc...    d_smythe32@aol.com
  Subject:  New Pair of Shoes

I am afraid the shoes I bought recently have fallen to pieces after
only two weeks.

I would like a full refund and look forward to receiving this in due
course.  I have already sent Ms. Smythe a copy of the receipt.

I look forward to a speedy reply.

Regards

Ms. J. Sherman
```

## 3.11.2 Formatting a Message

There are several different types of message you can set your system to send:

■ Plain Text displaying unformatted text.

■ Rich Text displaying some formatting.

■ HTML displaying messages just like web pages, showing images, links and coloured text.

To format a message:

1 *Click the Format menu.*

2 *Click Rich Text or HTML.*

3 *Use the formatting toolbar to emphasise selected text or apply different fonts and font sizes.*

4 *Click the Font option as an alternative to formatting the text.*

5 *Click the Paragraph option to realign text or add bullet points.*

![New Pair of Shoes - Message (Rich Text) email window showing the email editor with To, Cc, Subject fields and message body, with numbered callouts 2, 3, 4, 5 pointing to various interface elements and the Format menu open showing Font, Paragraph, Plain Text, Rich Text options]

The message body reads:

> I am afraid the shoes I bought recently have fallen to pieces after only two weeks.
>
> I would like a full refund and look forward to receiving this in due course. I have already sent Ms. Smythe a copy of the receipt.
>
> I look forward to a speedy reply.
>
> Regards
>
> *Ms. J. Sherman*

**Where do I put my own email address?**

Email systems add this detail automatically, so you do not need to add it yourself.

**3**

## 3.12  Copies

Assessment
Objective 3j

To send copies of an email to someone, complete the Cc: box with their full email address – for more than one person, separate the addresses with a semi-colon. These addresses will be visible to everyone receiving the message.

### 3.12.1 Blind Copies

Sometimes, you may want to send a copy of an email to someone without the recipient being aware of it. A common use for this facility is if you have a long mailing list but individuals may not want their email addresses visible to all the other people.

Keep these addresses private by adding a Bc: box and entering the address of the hidden recipient(s) here.

1. *Click the View menu.*

2. *Click BCC field.*

3. *Enter the address into the Bcc: box.*

4. *Send the message.*

> **Critical Error**
> Creating a second message rather than copying the original.

## 3.13 Saving Sent Messages

You need to show evidence that messages have been sent. If they do not appear in your Sent Items folder:

[1] *Click the Tools menu.*

[2] *Click Options.*

[3] *Click Email Options.*

[4] *Place a tick in the 'Save copies of messages...' box.*

[5] *Click OK.*

Save in Sent Items

## 3.14 Deleting Messages

**Assessment Objective 3k** Deleted messages are moved temporarily to the Deleted Items box, so they can be restored if you delete one by mistake. Once you empty the box, they will be lost completely.

### 3.14.1 Deleting

1. Click the message in the main window.

2. Press the Delete key.

Or

3. Click the Delete button ✕ on the toolbar.

Or

4. Right click and click Delete on the menu.

5. To remove messages permanently, right click the Deleted Items folder.

Or

6. Click the Tools menu.

7. Click 'Empty Deleted Items folder'.

## 3.15 Printing

**Assessment Objective 3i** You can print a message, an attachment and even contact email addresses.

When printing messages, your system may print just the message or include 'header' details. These can include the sender's name, the recipient's name, the subject of the message and the date it was sent. To make sure they are visible, always check printouts in Print Preview.

### What needs to be printed?

For New CLAIT, you must include header details as well as details of any attachments. If these are not visible on the printout, take a screen print of the message as well.

### ✕ Critical Error
**Missing printouts or no evidence of attachments on a printout.**

## 3.15.1 Printing Messages

1. *Click the message in the main window.*

2. *Click the print button to print a copy using default settings.*

Or

3. *Click the File menu.*

4. *Click Print Preview.*

5. *Check the message to make sure header details are visible.*

6. *Check that details of any attachments are visible.*

7. *Click the Print button.*

```
Print Preview                                          _ □ X

  [7]    ⊡ ⊡  ◎ ⊞ ⊞  ⬚ Page Setup...  ⬚ Print...  Close  ▶? .

         J. Sherman
         _____

  [5]    From:              J. Sherman
         Sent:              21 November 2005 15:34
         To:                'john@pearsoned-ema.com'
         Subject:           FW: Kitchens


  [6]              ⬚
                  kitchen.gif (76 KB)

                          Sarah sent this and I thought you might like to see

         Jackie

         -----Original Message-----
         From: J. Sherman
         Sent: 21 November 2005 15:27
         To: sarah@pearsoned-ema.com
         Cc: J. Sherman
         Subject: Kitchens


         Sarah

         I have been searching for useful web pages that will tell me ho
         kitchen.  I have found several and thought you might like to se

  1 Page
```

**I cannot see my messages in Print Preview**

Note that Print Preview may not be available for HTML formatted messages.

## 3.15.2 Printing Attachments

1. *Open the attachment.*

2. *Use the normal print options available. These will depend on the program you are using to view the file.*

Or

3. *Click the message showing in the main window.*

4. *Click the File menu.*

5. *Click Print.*

6. *Click to add a tick to the 'Print attached files' box.*

7. *Click OK.*

## 3.15.3 Printing Address Book Details

1. *Open Contacts.*

2. *Open the address you want to print.*

3. *Click the Print button.*

# Glossary

| | |
|---|---|
| **Alignment** | The position of entries – usually horizontally – on the page |
| **Application** | A software program used to carry out particular tasks |
| **Blind copy** | Sending a copy of an email to a recipient whose identity is hidden from others |
| **BODMAS** | The order in which mathematical calculations are performed |
| **Browser** | Software needed to view web pages |
| **Cell** | A square on a spreadsheet or in a table |
| **Cell reference** | Address of a spreadsheet cell using its column letter and row number |
| **Clip Art** | A gallery of pictures available for all Microsoft Office users |
| **Clipboard** | Part of the computer memory that stores files or objects temporarily.  Moving items out of the clipboard is known as pasting |
| **Composite printout** | All colours in a document printed together |
| **CPU** | Central Processing Unit – the 'brains' of the computer |
| **Default** | A setting that is applied automatically |
| **Demote** | Change to a lower level of text on a slide |
| **Domain name** | Location of a web page on the Internet indicating the type of organisation it belongs to |
| **Expression** | A combination of numbers, operators or variables representing an operation such as more than 5 (>5) |
| **Favourite** | Stored web page address for revisiting quickly |
| **Field** | Entry in a database stored in a specific category |
| **Folder** | A named area on a drive set aside for storing groups of similar files |
| **Font** | Style of character |
| **Footer** | Entries added at the bottom of a page in the margin area |
| **Formula** | Instruction on a spreadsheet to perform a calculation |
| **Forward** | To send on an email to a new recipient |
| **Function** | Pre-defined formula to carry out a specific calculation |

| | |
|---|---|
| **Function keys** | Keys at the top of the keyboard that act as shortcuts to specific dialog boxes |
| **Greyscale** | A tonal image encompassing black, white and shades of grey |
| **GUI** | Graphic User Interface – an easy way to work with a computer that makes use of windows, menus, icons and toolbars |
| **Header** | Entries added at the top of a page in the margin area |
| **Hexadecimal code** | The way colours on web pages are expressed |
| **History** | List of websites visited recently |
| **HTML** | HyperText Markup Language – the code used to write web pages |
| **Hyperlink** | Clickable text or image in a web page |
| **Inbox** | Email folder storing incoming messages |
| **Indenting** | Setting text away from the margin |
| **Internet** | Networks of computers linked across the world |
| **Justify** | An alignment that adds even word spacing to smooth left and right edges of a block of text |
| **Kerning** | Adjusting spaces between letters |
| **Landscape** | Page orientation with long sides top and bottom |
| **Master slide** | Slide containing items that will be displayed throughout a presentation |
| **Netiquette** | Code of conduct when communicating online |
| **Outbox** | Email folder storing outgoing messages until they are sent |
| **Pixels** | Individual coloured dots – picture elements – forming a bitmap or raster image |
| **Placeholder** | Shortcut on a slide to the addition of text or objects |
| **Portrait** | Page orientation with short sides top and bottom |
| **Primary key** | Unique identifier for one field in a database table |
| **Promote** | Change to a higher level of text on a slide |
| **Query** | Object created to search a database |
| **RAM** | Active memory (standing for Random Access Memory) |
| **Raster image** | Image made up of dots of colour – pixels |
| **Record** | All field entries for a single database item |
| **Resolution** | A measure of the number of pixels in an image |
| **RSI** | Repetitive Strain Injury – injury to some joints that is often caused by excessive computer use |
| **Sans serif** | Simpler styles of font without fine lines at the edges of the characters |

| | |
|---|---|
| **Search engine** | Website whose main activity is to provide a search facility |
| **Serif** | Font families with fine lines at the edge of the characters |
| **Sort** | Re-order numbers or records |
| **Template** | A ready-prepared document that can be used as a basis for creating your own files but leaves the original unchanged |
| **URL** | Web page address (Uniform Resource Locator) |
| **Vector image** | Image based on mathematical equations that stays sharp when scaled or rotated |
| **Virus** | Rogue program written to infect and interfere with the proper functioning of a computer |
| **Word wrap** | Text at the end of the line will be wrapped automatically onto the next line as you continue typing |
| **World Wide Web** | Multimedia pages published on the Internet |